Dedication

I dedicate this memoir to my late husband Bob Teahan and my deceased parents Joseph and Florence Keras. They believed in a just world and taught me important life lessons. They encouraged me to believe in myself, to believe in others, and to always have hope. My dedication also extends with love to my children, Anne, Jeanie, Bob, and John, their spouses, and my five grandchildren. Children are our future and our hope for a better world, and we must be the shoulders they stand on. "…we know that our inaction and inertia will be the inheritance of the next generation." (Twenty-two year-old Amanda Gorman's January 20, 2021, Inaugural Poem for our country)

Foreword by David Mulligan

When Hannah Arendt visited an aging Martin Buber in Jerusalem during the Eichmann Trial in1962, she was taken by his openness to different perspectives. "He is genuinely curious, desires to know and understand the world. In his 80th year he is more lively and receptive than all the opinionated dogmatists and know-it-alls. He has a definite sovereignty that pleases me." (Mendes-Flohr. Paul; Martin Buber, a Life of Faith and Dissent; Yale University Press, 2019.)

I have known Kathy Teahan for over 40 years and believe that the search for truth, like Buber's, has been a hallmark of her life. She has come to the truth by listening with love to the poor, the sick, and those in need. She sought the truth because she knew that it would cast a light on the injustices of our world. During her life, she has spoken truth to power. It is not easy to speak out for those in need because those in authority are often more interested in hearing from those with money, power. and influence.

As a member of the Catholic Church, Kathy has challenged the Church's position on women's reproductive rights and gay marriage. As a member of the legislature, she fought for healthcare for all, the treatment of those with alcohol and drug problems, needle exchange programs for addicts, increased services for the mentally ill, and support for gay marriage.

She learned that those in power did not like to be challenged. The Church harshly and publicly criticized this most Christian of women who courageously spoke from her heart. In her government experience, her unwillingness to accommodate the leadership often left her without the resources needed to serve her constituents—because to succeed in a worldly sense, one often needed to go along with those in power and ignore the problems of those in need. She did not seek wealth or power but sought to shine light on the truth and the needs of our poorest citizens.

One problem that she encountered in her church activity and in the legislature was that the power structure was dominated by men.

"THIS BOOK IS A MUST-READ FOR ALL WOMEN WHO ARE CONTEMPLATING A RUN FOR OFFICE."

"This memoir shows that despite the obstacles of big money and don't-rock-the-boat politics, it is possible to be a successful woman legislator. Rep. Kathy Teahan never gave up or gave in to the naysayers. Her determination and hard work brought many benefits to her constituents and to all Massachusetts citizens. This book is a must-read for all women who are contemplating a run for office.

Carol A. Donovan
State Representative-Woburn, 1991-2005

"Kathy Teahan's reflections on her ten years in the Massachusetts House of Representatives is a detailed recounting of her role in some of the momentous developments of our time: marriage equality, the rejection of the death penalty, and campaign finance reform. It is an intimate telling of the travails and joys of public life and of the struggles of a courageous, principled woman in the halls of power. And it is a call for us—electeds and citizens alike—to do better. Too many of us don't vote. Not enough of us run for office. Members of the House surrender too much of their authority and power to the Speaker. Money plays a corrupting role in the public square, shaping who runs, who wins, and what they do once in office. Ms. Teahan doesn't just list problems. She poses solutions. In this telling, as in her decade in office, Ms. Teahan makes clear that she has lived up to her formal title, the Honorable Kathleen Teahan."

Jay R. Kaufman
State Representative-Lexington, 1995-2019
Beacon Leadership Collaborative, Founding President

"HER MEMOIR IS PARTLY A GUIDE TO THE ARDUOUS PROCESS OF RUNNING FOR OFFICE, PARTLY A REVELATION OF THE CYNICISM AND DYSFUNCTIONALITY THAT UNDERMINE THE INSTITUTIONS CHARGED WITH PROMOTING THE COMMON GOOD..."

"Rep. Kathleen Teahan's *For the People, Against the Tide* is a must-read for anyone seeking to understand what is broken in government, and what kinds of change are needed to make it work "for the people." I had the honor of serving with Rep Teahan in the Massachusetts House, where I quickly came to admire her pure devotion to public service. Her memoir is partly a guide to the arduous process of running for office, partly a revelation of the cynicism and dysfunctionality that undermine the institutions charged with promoting the common good – in this case, the Massachusetts House of Representatives. Since its systemic flaws are not unique to it, this book has a universal application. Rep. Teahan shows us how power structures and customs can undermine democracy, and obstruct even elected leaders from doing the work that voters elect them to do. It's the kind of book we urgently need at this point in the history of our nation."

Denise Provost
State Representative-Somerville, 2006-2021

"An honest and forthright journey for Kathy Teahan from motherhood and being a teacher with high humanistic standards and values, to entering the complex and competing agendas of the political worlds of money, power, bureaucracies and the state legislature. It's complicated and often discouraging, many people suffer unnecessarily, but persistence and high standards can make a difference... Kathy Teahan, a voice for the voiceless, kept her standards and made a difference...a must read."

Myron Allukian, Jr.,DDs,MPH
Former Dental Director, City of Boston
Past President, American Public Health Association

For the People, Against the Tide: A Democratic Woman's Ten Years in the Massachusetts Legislature

By Kathleen Teahan

(D-Whitman)

ISBN: 978-1-7376985-2-4

Cover Design and Book Design/Layout
by Pamela Johnson, Techpro Publications
www.TechproPublications.com

A just, curious, and humane community will never be realized unless the voices of all are lovingly and equally heard.

How did this listening Kathy Teahan respond to the setbacks she experienced? After retirement she moved to the Cape, volunteered at a soup kitchen and at a Reiki clinic for cancer patients, and offered driving services for patients going to clinics. She continues to dedicate her time to make this world a better place for the less fortunate.

Why does she do these things? I believe that she thinks that every day is important and that we are called at every stage of our life to be open to the suffering of the world. With this knowledge of the truth, we must act. She is motivated by a spiritual, a universal and transcendent spirit that sees that we must overcome the oppressions of gender, class, ethnicity, race, and religion if we are to achieve the possibility of the happiness of all in this world.

If you believe that all people deserve happiness and wish to be motivated to participate in this goal, read this book and be exposed to a Kathy who works for this dream every day. As she learned more about the world, she changed her views. The changes were based on her empathy for the people that she met on her journey. They were changes from the heart.

She has a sovereignty that pleases me. It is based on being open to the world.

David H. Mulligan
Massachusetts Commissioner of Public Health (1989-1997)

Foreward by Dr. Howard K. Koh

When I first entered government as the Massachusetts Commissioner of Public Health, I was uncertain what public service might have in store. So many warned me, a long-practicing physician and a newcomer to politics, to be wary of anyone in the State House. I steeled myself to be ready for anything. But meeting Representative

Kathy Teahan utterly disarmed me. From our very first interaction, she stunned me with her profound humility and humanity. Time and again, I witnessed how she tirelessly sought common ground among warring factions and found ways for everyone to work together to protect the precious and fragile gift of health. Others would regularly argue, lecture, or pontificate—but not Kathy. Whether listening attentively to small groups of constituents in her office or addressing large public gatherings before her Joint Committee on Public Health, she always exhibited steadfast passion and great compassion. She was the calm in the storm, always embodying the mission of service to the underserved.

Seeing her in action, I was constantly amazed how she, an elected official forced to endure the grueling hardships of endless fundraising and bruising campaigns, could yet conduct herself with such gentle dignity. But that was the source of Kathy's soft power. She unfailingly treated each person, regardless of background or status, with unqualified respect. And whenever she asked any of us for advice or support, we always dug down deep to deliver our best effort. Because we never wanted to let her down.

Over the years since our time together, Kathy's example has stayed with me—first through federal government service in the Obama Administration and now as a public health professor. I am delighted to celebrate her memoir that richly describes a life of dedication and purpose. Representative Kathy Teahan's story is one of tireless concern for all and a passionate belief that public service is both an honor and a solemn responsibility. Her remarkable history demonstrates that government leaders can truly lead lives that make a difference.

Howard K. Koh, MD, MPH
Massachusetts Commissioner of Public Health, 1997-2003
U.S. Assistant Secretary for Health, 2009-2014
Professor of the Practice of Public Health Leadership, Harvard
TH Chan School of Public Health and Harvard Kennedy School

Author's Note

"There comes a time when silence is betrayal," said Dr. Martin Luther King—words that we've heard a lot since the death of George Floyd on May 25, 2020.

When I left the Massachusetts Legislature in 2007, after serving the people of Whitman, Abington, and East Bridgewater for ten years, I felt I had unfinished responsibilities remaining for the well-being of my constituents. I had loved my work as a legislator, but after ten years with only one aide, I couldn't adequately answer all the calls for help we received, nor could I attend fully to important policy and budget matters. In 2008, attempting to finish fulfilling my duties to the people of Massachusetts, I enrolled in a memoir class, hoping that by sharing my experiences, I would inspire others to learn more about our government and to get involved in whatever way they could. In 2020, witnessing the growing heartache of Americans and others around the world due to what I perceived as an inept federal U. S. government, I could no longer be silent. The time had come to complete my memoir.

Being a state representative is a great honor that comes with great responsibility. I remember the first time I picked up mail addressed to The Honorable Kathleen M. Teahan. The title connoted a pretty distinguished position! People at the State House called me Representative Teahan or the more familiar, "Rep." State House staff went out of their way to help me and always treated me with respect. It was an honor to know that the people in my district trusted me to make decisions in their best interests. Being one of the 219 women ever elected to serve in the Massachusetts Legislature, in contrast to the more than 20,000 men who have served, is still quite a privilege. (These statistics for the year 2020, the One Hundredth Anniversary of Women's Suffrage, speak for themselves!)

In 1997, when I took the oath of office in the House Chamber of the Massachusetts State House, I believed I could make a positive difference in the lives of Massachusetts residents. With my right hand raised, I repeated, "I, Kathleen M. Teahan, do solemnly swear that I will bear true faith and allegiance to the Commonwealth of Massachusetts, and will support the Constitution thereof. So help me God." I believed that as a member of the majority party, and a Democrat, I would work with leadership to fulfill our responsibilities for providing justice, protecting workers, funding outstanding educational opportunities for all, providing accessible and affordable health care, protecting our environment, and addressing the needs of our disabled and elderly. I realized that other legislators would have different opinions about how to achieve our goals; but I believed that through debates and compromises, we'd be voices for the hard-working, tax-paying people of our districts.

I was surprised to learn that this wouldn't actually be the case!

I was honored and excited every day of the decade I spent serving the people of Massachusetts; and yet, the disappointments abounded. The following were but a few.

When answering a request from my constituent suffering with breast cancer, I couldn't believe the automatic denial of Social Security benefits to her and to others with legitimate serious diseases. This forty-three-year-old woman, who had worked for years as a dental hygienist and had paid her taxes, had to expend the precious energy, so needed to fight her cancer, on making phone calls, filling out endless forms, and appealing repeated denials for unemployment insurance when she could not work. Getting through the government bureaucracy should never be this burdensome.

What a disappointment it was to learn that the U.S. Securities and Exchange Commission ignored my constituent, Harry Markopolos, who blew the whistle on Bernie Madoff in 2004. As a result of Madoff's fifty-billion-dollar Ponzi scheme, many people lost their life savings, their homes, and their retirement money; and many non-profits and foundations lost resources for helping those in need. But no one had listened to Harry Markopolos. (Massachusetts Secretary of State William Galvin, and New York's Attorneys General Andrew

Cuomo and Eliot Spitzer did try to do the job our federal government wasn't doing.)

It was also a disappointment to realize there were loopholes in our legislation providing tax breaks to retain for-profit companies like Fidelity and Raytheon and the jobs they provided for our workers. These loopholes allowed companies receiving tax breaks to leave the state without consequences to their bottom line. Those companies, feeling no fealty to Massachusetts, were leaving the Commonwealth permanently despite the tax breaks they had received. This is just one example of the corporate welfare provided by Massachusetts and throughout our country on both state and federal levels. Today, it is unconscionable that at least sixty of America's largest companies paid no taxes on their collective $79 billion in profits in 2018. (Amazon was one of those sixty companies, and it pays me all of $1.73 when it sells my children's book, *The Cookie Loved 'Round the World*, to the public for $14.95.) Tax breaks, loopholes in the tax laws, and low corporate tax rates continue to enable this imbalance and empower these companies.

Then there was the issue of privatization. You might be as surprised as I was to learn that many government services have now been privatized because private companies see our government's billions of dollars as opportunities to increase their own profits. Our prison-industrial complex is one example. Thanks to Representative Kay Khan (D-Newton) a former psychiatric nurse, I visited several prisons in Massachusetts and learned a lot about privatization of corrections facilities from social justice advocates. Even in government-run facilities, food service, healthcare, laundry, and cleaning are provided, often without oversight, by private companies. Many inmates in this privatized prison system are low-income, nonviolent offenders, the mentally ill, and people of color. One out of every five people incarcerated in the U. S. is today guilty of low-level drug charges, like first time possession. (PBS World News, September 24, 2020) Keeping prisons full is keeping the prison industry profitable.

Living only twenty miles from Plymouth, I was (and still am) concerned about the danger presented by the Pilgrim Nuclear Power Plant. As a member of Will/WAND (Women's Legislative Lobby/ Women for New Direction) I learned about regulatory agencies, such as the Nuclear Regulatory Commission (NRC) that oversaw safety at the Pilgrim plant but seemed to protect industries more than the safety of citizens. If Attorney General Maura Healy had not sued the NRC before the decommissioning and transfer of the Pilgrim plant to Holtec International, there would still have been far fewer citizen protections in the 2019 agreement.

I was also surprised and disappointed to see controversial legislation placed in the Outside Sections of the annual state budget in order to circumvent the open legislative process. The Outside Sections were meant to "clarify" appropriation line items in the budget *before* they were voted on. In each annual budget, there often were a couple hundred "outside sections," some of which included legislation that, without hearings or debate, became laws. Unfortunately, some of these Outside Sections also hid support for special interests. An example was the legislation enabling a questionable Connecticut non-profit to receive a percentage of the Massachusetts 9/11 license plate revenues.

Despite my disappointments in the reality of how our state and federal governments operated, I am still hopeful for the future of our American democracy. I loved being a legislator, loved the people in my district, and loved the people I met as a legislator. Most politicians I met, both Democrats and Republicans, were good people who cared about our Commonwealth of Massachusetts. However, the broken political system, mostly due to misuse of power and money, reduces the political will needed to legislate in the best interests of the people of the Commonwealth. Since the beginning of our democratic government, many powerful politicians have granted special favors to those who would help them retain their power. Unfortunately, what I saw happening and continue to see increasing every year is that money and power (the desire for individual power and the maintenance of power by political parties) are decreasing our opportunities for bettering the lives of the hard-working middle class and the economically disadvantaged. We need to start seeing ourselves and each other not as Democrats or Republicans, but as Americans. Listening carefully and respectfully to those whose opinions differ from our own is essential. I remain a Democrat because I believe in the values of the Democratic party, but both parties must make service to the people of the Commonwealth their priority.

Inspired by Congressman John Lewis's memorable words, "If you see something that is not right, not fair, not just, you have to say something, you have to do something," this book—a legislator's memoir, in truth— is my gift to the people of Massachusetts and people throughout the world. We are all in this together.

If my generation doesn't pass on what we learned to the next generation, our children's children will continue to make the same mistakes we did. Some will suffer needlessly from preventable and treatable diseases, some will be left to live on our streets or be forgotten in our prisons, and some will be maimed or die in unnecessary wars. We have to imagine the world we want to leave for our children.

Like Gandhi, I believe that we must "be the change we want for this world." This memoir is my small contribution to a more just and peaceful world for our children, our grandchildren, and for all who come after us.

Table of Contents

Chapter 1: My Path to Politics

As I look back on my decision in 1995 to run for the open state representative seat for Abington, East Bridgewater, and Whitman, I remember the shy, quiet child, the insecure, awkward adolescent, and the somewhat unworldly young woman I was before my decade-long career in politics. Politics and leadership had never much interested me and certainly were not among my aspirations before 1995.

But they became my passion.

I was born in 1947, the first-born of Joe and Florence (Mahoney) Keras. My father Josef Keras, the son of Lithuanian immigrants, worked forty hours a week, fifty weeks a year over a sweltering fire, pouring molten iron into molds in the Whitman Foundry. He was a strong man with muscular arms and legs. At home he was a quiet man who would sit evenings at our kitchen table (a picnic table with benches) and listen to news radio programs. On weekends, he had a few beers, enjoyed playing with us, socializing with neighbors, and teasing my mother.

When I was in high school, I learned from a classmate who worked part-time at the foundry that my dad used the foulest language imaginable when things went wrong at work. In contrast, he never even said "shut up" at home. I was shocked to hear this, but when I realized the vulgar language was a release of the pain my father endured as a molder, I was proud of his respect for our family evidenced by his choice of language at home with us. At night, before bed, my dad would sit at his bedroom window inhaling fresh air and coughing out the black soot that invaded his lungs each day at the foundry.

My mother, Florence Keras, had been named the prettiest girl in her Franklin High School Class of '42 yearbook. Her dream was to have a big, happy family. She left her hairdressing career to raise eight children, sewing matching outfits for us when we were still a family of four little girls. Later, when there were six girls and two boys in the family, Mom made coats, hats, prom gowns, and wedding gowns for us and for her granddaughters. She often spent her "club" money (a weekly prepaid amount of money to the store for future purchases) at Sally's Dress Shop in downtown Whitman for a back-to-school or other special outfit for one of her six daughters. After all these years, we continue to be a happy and loving family of eight siblings and our extended families.

As a family, we went to Mass every Sunday, visited relatives often, and didn't own a car until 1964. When I got my driver's license that year, a friend of my mother's cousin Lucy gave me a car that had a hole in the floor large enough to put a foot through. This car provided me a way to practice my driving, run errands, and feel less ashamed of always relying on relatives and neighbors for rides.

My parents, seven siblings, and I, along with my widowed grandmother, Helen (Wall) Mahoney, lived in an eight-room, colonial-style home with one and a half baths on Brigham Street in Whitman, Massachusetts. At times during my college, teaching, and legislative years, I thought that if I had grown up in an environment where world issues, politics, literature, and the arts had been discussed more often, I would have been better prepared for success in life. However, during a retreat at St. Joseph's Manor in Cohasset, in 2005, as I sat in silence at a window looking out at a blue sky and a calm ocean, I realized it was the unconditional love and self-sacrificing support my parents had given me that provided the strength I needed to stand up for those who didn't have a voice and do things I never imagined I could.

An early entry into politics

My first step toward my political career happened in the fourth grade. *Weekly Reader Magazine* was holding a mock election and I was trying to decide who would get my vote, Dwight Eisenhower or Adlai Stevenson. When I asked my parents for help, they told me that Stevenson was a Democrat and that Democrats represented working class families and helping the needy. Even as a nine-year-old, I knew I was a Democrat. I voted for the Democrat, Adlai Stevenson, and I have been a Democrat ever since.

The only memory I have of any reference to a political career was when my father, who enjoyed a good debate, would argue different issues with me and say that I'd make a good politician because I liked to argue. While I have never particularly enjoyed disagreeing with others, I couldn't remain quiet when I thought they were wrong. I often have felt compelled to stand up for what I believed in, especially when it came to protecting my family or others in need. As a preteen, I ran down the street after two six-foot-tall adolescent boys who were bothering my younger sisters. Later in life, as a married woman, I stood up against most of my neighbors at a zoning board meeting to speak in favor of a proposal for converting a large home in our neighborhood to a state-run residential home for persons with disabilities.

When I graduated from Whitman-Hanson Regional High School in 1965, most girls were limited to career choices as secretaries, teachers, nurses, or housewives. I majored in English and minored in education and history while attending Bridgewater State College (now University), just seven miles down Route 18 from my home in Whitman. In August of 1969, Dr. E. Harry Boothby, Superintendent of the Whitman-Hanson Regional School District came to my summer workplace, Sally's Dress Shop, to discuss an open teaching position at Whitman-Hanson Regional High School, my alma mater. He had one stipulation before hiring me for the English position: I had to also accept a position as the cheerleading coach. I wasn't athletic and knew nothing about cheerleading, but we decided the girls on the squad could teach each other the cheers, and my responsibility would be ensuring their safety and behavior. Who would have thought that this would become part of my path to politics!

Teaching, and meeting Bob Teahan

Teaching was a challenge for me. I had been a hardworking, over-achieving student, yet was still somewhat introverted. I really cared about my students and wanted to succeed, so I worked hard to prepare good lessons and make learning interesting. I was also anxious to get married and have children. When Dana Nash, a twenty-three-year-old man from Abington, whom I had been dating, surprised me with an engagement ring during his holiday leave from the U. S. Army, I was happy. Although I wasn't sure I was ready to commit to marriage, I accepted. Maybe I felt pressure because my younger sister and my two best friends were engaged.

About three months after my engagement, I joined a group of teachers playing in a faculty/student basketball game at Whitman-Hanson Regional High School to raise money for high school athletics. A dozen or so teachers went to the Alamo Restaurant in Abington for drinks and appetizers after the game. At the piano bar, Bob Benoit, a local entertainer, was playing "The Tennessee Waltz," and the head of the Social Studies Department asked me to dance. I danced with him but didn't feel comfortable because he was married, so I said, "You know who I'd really like to dance with? Your friend, Mr. Teahan."

Bob Teahan was a recent widower, the athletic director, the head football coach, and the physical education director at Whitman-Hanson. He was sitting at the bar with Bob O'Connell, a Brockton teacher and football coach, and his wife Ann. We stopped dancing, and I asked Mr. Teahan to dance. Holding his mug of draft beer at the circular bar, he smiled and answered, "I have a wooden leg and don't dance." But, I knew he didn't have a wooden leg and somehow his smile and his manner intrigued me. I guess my request for a dance somehow also intrigued Bob. From that night on, when the football coaches went out socially, the assistant coaches invited some of the women coaches, including me as the cheerleading coach. With encouragement from his assistant coaches, I always sat beside Mr.

Teahan. More and more I was attracted to this older yet physically fit man who had accomplished so much in his life. I knew I'd have to face hurting Dana by breaking off our engagement, but my feelings for Bob became a love that I couldn't ignore.

Bob grew up in Holyoke, Massachusetts. When he was only eight years old, his father died. Bob's mother, Cora, had three young children: Bob, his sister Mary, his brother Edward, and an unborn baby Donald, who died shortly after birth. After Bob's father's death, close family friends took Bob under their wings and invited him to many sporting events. As a result, baseball, basketball, swimming, football, and all athletics became Bob's passion, and that passion became his vocation as a physical education teacher, coach, athletic director, and later a professional football scout for the New England Patriots. He was a World War II veteran who served on the frontlines in Germany. He was respected throughout the South Shore as an outstanding high school and semi-pro football coach, and he had developed a boys' physical education program that was written up in the Boston Globe's magazine section.

By spring 1970, Bob and I were together more and more. I'd "just happen" to be in my Aunt Helen Vaughan's backyard on Jenkins Avenue, adjacent to the Mt. Zion Cemetery where Bob worked an after-school job preparing the cemetery for Memorial Day. We'd chat and I'd bring him homemade cookies or other goodies. By mid-summer we had both broken our previous wedding engagements. Yes, Bob was also engaged to someone else when we fell in love. In fact, they had already had their wedding invitations printed, and Bob's home was being renovated to accommodate his fiancé's taste. In spite of the pain our fiancés endured because of our decisions, I still feel we did the right thing for all involved. Bob had two daughters, Anne, thirteen, and Jeanie, ten. They were very friendly and welcoming when I visited, even though they were probably confused by all the recent changes in their lives—the loss of their young mother to cancer and their father's change in wedding plans.

One weekend Bob invited his brother Ed's family to a cookout, and I was there having fun in the pool with Anne and Jeanie. Ed saw me and said, "Who's Anne's [Bob's daughter] new friend in the pool?" Other people were even more outspoken about their uneasiness with our age difference. A couple who had been friends of Jean, Bob's first wife, told Bob he was being very foolish and severed their relationships with him. Both my parents and Bob were very nervous the first time we all went out together that summer. I'm sure many people in town were talking about us. Still, Bob and I dated all summer and into the fall.

Back at school, Bob and I often met in the library around 7 a.m., before classes started. He would affectionately tap my head with his newspaper as he walked by the table where I sat grading papers. That was the extent of any public display of our affection. When I chaperoned the cheerleaders as they decorated the boys' locker room on Friday nights before the football games, I was as excited as they were, and yet I never expressed anything but school pride and spirit with them.

Bob gave me an engagement ring in November of 1970. So our news would not distract players from the big Abington/Whitman-Hanson Thanksgiving football game, I kept this beautiful diamond ring in my bureau drawer until after Thanksgiving. Then, I proudly wore his ring through the holiday season, and we married on February 12, 1971. Bob was fifty years old, and I was almost twenty-four.

Bob and I had twenty-six happy years of marriage with not one boring day. Our personalities complemented each other's, and we both encouraged and supported each other's dreams. Because of this, we both lived full and happy lives. Since Bob was a "night person" and I was a "morning person," he often wrote me late-night notes on paper plates and napkins after his midnight snacks. Notes were his comments on current affairs, issues before the legislature, or inspirational speeches.

Bob joins the legislature

People in our community really looked up to Bob. He inspired hundreds of young men in his physical education classes and on his teams to believe in themselves and accomplish more than they felt they could. Many wrote to him later in life about his impact on their success and happiness. Shortly after our marriage, I discovered my husband was very interested in history and politics, in addition to football and coaching. This discovery really sank in when he asked what I thought about his running for an open state representative's seat for our district in 1973. (He was always considerate about me and our children when making decisions.) I knew nothing about political life but told him that if it were important to him, it was fine with me.

And so began my introduction to politics.

Aided by our two daughters, Anne and Jeanie, then fifteen and twelve, our two-year-old son Bobby, and a great group of volunteers, I set out to help him get elected in a very hard-fought campaign against a small business owner and well-known town selectman, Al Clayton.

Bob won this first race, and he won again two years later. However, at the end of his second term, the Massachusetts House did some major redistricting that reduced the number of House seats from 240 to 160. He had enjoyed representing his district and its many families, but the redistricting would require him to run against Paul Moriarty, a fellow Democrat whom he respected. This new larger district would involve more campaigning and attending more district events. Bob finally decided not to run for a third term. Instead, he became a full-time scout for the New England Patriots professional football team, scouting college players for nearly twenty years.

Bob's interest in politics never ended, but the needs of our family took precedence, and he devoted his time and energy to work and family. Our second son John was born in 1976, Bob's second year in the legislature. In 1979, my stepdaughter Anne married R. Emmet Hayes, Bob's former football captain who had also served as Bob's campaign manager. Jeanie was at UMass Dartmouth studying business and marketing, and Bobby was a fun and imaginative six-year-old. From 1973 to 1983, I was a stay-at-home mom, busy with family matters and community service. Beginning in 1979, as Bob traveled the East Coast evaluating college athletes as prospective Patriots players, I decided (with Bob's encouragement) to run for and was elected to the Whitman School Committee.

The day after I was elected, Wally Benson, the father of a former W-H-R (Whitman-Hanson Regional High School) football player, said to me, "Enjoy your popularity today because after your first vote, some people will disagree with you." Being an elected official is not for the faint of heart, but Bob and I believed that quality education was the key to a better life for the next generation and a better world for all. Our dear neighbor Elaine Bergeron, who became a life-long friend, took care of our young sons on school committee nights.

Deciding to run for state office

While not working at a paying job, I volunteered: in my sons' elementary school classrooms, as a religious education teacher, a Eucharistic minister, and member of the parish council at Holy Ghost Roman Catholic Church. I was a member of the Whitman Democratic Town Committee, a volunteer for Habitat for Humanity, an outreach worker for the homebound, and an active worker on our local scholarship committee. During the years from 1978 until 1995, my involvement in politics was minimal. From 1987 to 1995, I was a full-time middle school teacher.

In April 1995, things changed. Plymouth County District Attorney William O'Malley died, and our state representative, Michael Sullivan, was appointed by Governor Bill Weld to fill the vacancy created by O'Malley's death. As a result, the state representative seat opened up for our district, which included the three small towns along Route 18 on the South Shore: Abington, Whitman, and East Bridgewater.

One April morning, Bob and I stood in front of Duval's Pharmacy, one of the few remaining independent drug stores in our area, chatting about this open seat with Emmet Hayes, our former son-in-law and our former state representative (1980-1990). During the conversation, Emmet said to Bob, "Now's your chance to make a comeback into politics." And without really thinking, I said, "If anyone from this family runs, it will be me." Bob and Emmet looked at each other and Bob said, "Kathy, you'd really like being a rep. You love helping people, and as a rep, you'd be in a position to do a lot of good."

Later, as Bob and I continued our discussion about the open seat, he pointed out that representatives influence policies that could improve life for the, then, six million people in Massachusetts. This was pretty heady stuff for someone who was then teaching seventh and eighth grade English at the East Bridgewater Middle School (later to become the Gordon W. Mitchell Middle School). It was April and I would have to make a decision soon in order to organize a campaign committee and turn in nomination papers in June. Speaker Thomas Finneran and the legislature had set the primary election for August 22, 1995, and the special election for the open seat for September 19, 1995. I gave myself until Mother's Day to decide.

Decision-making meant composing the following list of the pros and cons involved in a possible run:

Pro: I wanted to be in a position to make good policies for our state.

Con: I needed to learn about many issues that were unfamiliar to me.

Pro: My years of volunteerism showed my dedication to the community.

Con: I didn't like giving speeches or being in the limelight.

Pro: I had lived my entire life in this community and my large extended family would help and support me.

Con: Asking for money and volunteer help was not something I wanted to do.

Pro: This would be an exciting challenge and a change of career.

Con: Campaigns were costly, and Bob and I were making a modest living and would need to do a lot of fundraising to pay for the campaign.

As I considered a run, I reached out to community activists in the district, other Democrats who might be considering a run, and heads of the Massachusetts Democratic Party. For some reason, I kept watching the *Forest Gump* video during those weeks. Perhaps it was the "Run, Forest, Run" lines that moved me, or maybe it was simply the way Forest overcame so many odds while trying to help others. On Mother's Day, I told my family and friends I had decided to campaign for the Seventh Plymouth District House of Representatives seat. We held my campaign kick-off on June 27, 1995, at the Whitman Knights of Columbus Hall, a metal building on Route 18 in Whitman. My knees were quite shaky as I delivered that first speech.

Four Democrats ran in that primary. All three of my Democratic opponents were men from East Bridgewater. (See Appendix 1.) On the Republican side, three other male candidates wanted the seat (See Appendix 2.) We were quite a mix of personalities and backgrounds, and our relationships were interconnected in several ways.

As a mother, a Eucharistic minister at Holy Ghost Church, and a middle school teacher in East Bridgewater, I didn't want to embarrass my children, my Church, or my students with a nasty, negative campaign. I wanted to give people the issues-centered campaign most voters yearned for, and I didn't want to be divisive or antagonistic toward people whose families and friends I had known in our community. I told my campaign volunteers we were going to run a positive campaign, and after learning what each candidate offered in experience, attitude, and vision, voters would decide on the best person to serve as their new state representative. I would present my qualifications, my stands on issues, and my plans for helping the district, and we would show voters that campaigns could be amicable and positive.

Boy was I in for a surprise!

Chapter 2: The Nuts & Bolts of Political Campaigns

The almighty lawn sign

"Sledge and Stake" were nicknames given to my husband Bob and his friend Don Monahan for the sledgehammer and iron stake they used to securely anchor my campaign lawn signs during my 1995 and 1996 campaigns. These signs were fourteen inches high and twenty-eight inches long, printed in a union shop on glossy cardboard stock. In goldenrod-yellow large block letters, my name TEAHAN stood out on a grass-green background. Below the TEAHAN, in white script, were the words "Kathleen for State Representative, Abington, East Bridgewater and Whitman." The cardboard was stapled to heavy two-by-four wooden frames. In his basement, my Uncle Bob Mahoney made and repaired hundreds of my signs, and local carpenter unions made and donated hundreds more for me and other Democrats who received their union endorsements.

Bob and Don were a mostly two-man lawn sign committee during my first campaign. Don was a gregarious guy who was active in the Whitman Knights of Columbus and a passionate booster of youth and school sports. He had a heart of gold and knew thousands of people in our district. And Bob, the popular former football coach, state representative, and New England Patriots football scout, while not as outgoing as Don, was highly respected, and people enjoyed talking with him.

I was lucky to have the support of many well-known and respected people in the community whose endorsements increased my credibility as a political candidate. Beth Hayes, who coordinated my East Bridgewater campaigns, had spearheaded the building of a new addition to the middle school, and Shawn Reilly and Kathy Kennedy, who ran my Abington campaigns, were leaders in the building of a new town hall and library. All three were highly regarded, active volunteers in their hometowns. Surrounding yourself with experienced, knowledgeable, honest, and caring advisers was and is important to a successful campaign as well as to good leadership thereafter.

Lawn signs are a daily reminder to voters that an election is approaching. They create name recognition and imply voter support. The right lawn-sign strategy can build momentum, so important in campaigns. My campaign advisers had stressed the importance of asking voters for permission to place lawn signs in their yards as I canvassed neighborhoods and knocked on doors asking for votes. Going door-to-door, I recorded favorable voter responses with "yes" on a paper voter list that I carried, and I used an S to signify a permitted sign location.

These were the days before iPads, tablets, and other electronic devices were available for campaigns. During that first campaign, in a rush to meet as many people as possible as I went door-knocking, my notes weren't always clear. (As you read further, you'll learn the consequences.) Time constraints demanded that I concentrate on contacting as many voters as possible during the day, and on attending meetings, making phone calls, and studying the issues each night.

(Back, L-R): Kathy's parents, Joseph & Florence Keras; Kathy & Bob; Anne Teahan & Bill Berry; (front): Kathy's nieces, nephews and granddaughter Jill Hayes

My first street lists of voter responses went, without my checking my symbols and my hastily-written sloppy notes, to Terrie Craven, a volunteer typing the lawn-sign list. Consequently, one late autumn afternoon as I drove home after a long day of knocking on doors, there were perky fourteen-by-twenty-eight-inch yellow and green Teahan lawn signs on almost every yard in my Harvard Street neighborhood. To my weary eyes, Harvard Street looked like the field of daffodils from the movie *Dr. Zhivago*! I had to make a lot of calls that night to apologize to families about the unexpected signs on their lawns. Surprisingly, we gained a few new sign locations through the mistaken "yes for support" versus the "yes for a lawn sign" on the list. (Another lawn sign incident occurred a couple of campaigns later when, during a rainstorm, the print on my less expensive signs totally washed away. Those signs had to be reprinted, reassembled, and replaced!)

As my campaign committee and I gained experience, we developed a very successful lawn-sign strategy that helped win elections. As noted earlier, building momentum is important to winning elections. To the dismay of some nervous volunteers and supporters who saw our opponents' signs going up around the district, we held back placing our signs outdoors until two weeks before the primary. Then, we flooded the neighborhoods with our signs, and that caught the attention of voters. The last campaign of my career (2004) saw the transition to newly designed signs that were easily stapled over a wire frame. (Both "Sledge" and "Stake" had died several years earlier and along with them, the era of those cumbersome wooden lawn signs.) Today, campaign lawn signs are plastic sleeves or corrugated plastic that fit over wire frames. (My son Bobby, who became a member of the new lawn-sign committee, said, with his usual dry humor, that the new signs had revolutionized campaigns, so now, because placing signs didn't require extreme arm strength, women could be on the lawn sign committees!)

The crucial campaign budget

Money, and a well-organized committee with a rolodex of volunteer information, and later, excel spreadsheets and electronic databases on iPads, became necessary for a political campaign. A clear delivery of my message and a willingness to give 110% to the campaign were other essential components to a successful campaign.

Financing the campaign was enormously important in order to pay for strategists; lawn signs; printing and mailing of brochures; postage; websites; TV, newspaper and radio ads; and tickets to community functions. To raise money, my committee ran dances, cocktail parties, and movie nights. I filled out questionnaires and answered questions at endorsement sessions to request funds from labor unions, from social worker, nurse, and teachers-union PACs (Political Action Committees), and from other groups.

Bob and I were both working then, and we earned a total of close to $100,000 a year during my first campaign. I loaned the first campaign about $20,000 and we raised $30,000. After Bob died in 1997, I made $50,000—$55,000 a year as a full-time legislator.

Living in a predominantly blue-collar town, I was able to campaign successfully with moderate expenditures. My campaign committee and I raised and spent approximately $30-40,000 during each of my four campaigns for re-election. Some candidates for state legislative seats—statewide positions as well as congressional seats—spend hundreds

Kathy's late husband Robert S. Teahan, State Representative from Whitman (1976—1979)

~ 32 ~

of thousands, even millions of dollars of their own money on campaigns. (See Appendix 3.) Some elected state officials had and still have hundreds of thousands of dollars, and even millions, reserved in their campaign accounts, or "war chests," which discouraged opponents because opponents who weren't independently wealthy would need to spend a lot of time raising money to level the campaign-spending field.

Delivering the message

Organization was critical for Getting Out the Vote (GOTV) and carrying out the various campaign strategies in an effective time frame. I found knocking on doors and talking to people to be one of the most effective strategies in my campaigns. Voters appreciated a candidate who took the time to personally answer their questions and ask for their vote. Also, leaving a brochure on their doorknobs with a "Sorry I missed you" note let them know I had been in the neighborhood to see them when they

Losing Bob in September 1997, only nine months after he attended my swearing-in ceremony in the House Chamber, suddenly changed my life. Bob had been my campaign manager, my mentor, my emotional support, and my soulmate. He was the parent who brought laughter and fun to my four children and me. Now, as a widow, campaigning every other year and maintaining my home, in addition to working full-time as a legislator, was hard work. I didn't mind the work because, as Bob had told me I would, I loved my job helping people, and it kept my mind off my loss (except for Friday nights, when tears came).

The day before his September 12, 1997, death from pulmonary thrombosis, Bob had left a note for me on the kitchen table before he headed to the Cape to enjoy a weekend with his brother Ed. Written on a paper plate, it read: "KMT – Thank you for making me happy every day. I didn't know that life could be so happy. Thank you for being you. I love you very, very much.—RST." This cherished note filled me with gratitude for the happiness we shared and a desire that all people have happy lives with loved ones.

Don't Quit

When things go wrong, as they
  sometimes will,
When the road you're trudging seems
  all uphill,
When the funds are low and the debts
  are high,
And you want to smile but you have
  to sigh,
When care is pressing you down
  a bit —
Rest if you must, but don't you quit.

Life is queer with its twists and turns,
As every one of us sometimes learns,
And many a fellow turns about,
When he might have won had he
  stuck it out.
Don't give up though the pace seems
  slow —
You may succeed with another blow.

Often the goal is nearer than
It seems to a faint and faltering man;
Often the struggler has given up
When he might have captured the
  victor's cup,
And he learned too late when the night
  came down,
How close he was to the golden crown.

Success is failure turned inside out —
The silver tint of the clouds of doubt,
And you never can tell how close you
  are,
It may be near when it seems afar;
So stick to the fight when you're
  hardest hit, —
It's when things seem worst that you
  mustn't quit.

Author unknown

Compliments of
Kathleen Teahan
State Representative
⊕ 75

*Bookmark Distributed
for Kathy's Campaign*

were not at home. Besides brochures, I gave out bookmarks with the "Don't Quit" poem, which I later learned was used by Alcoholics Anonymous. People of all ages kept that poem on their mirrors or beside their beds to read during those trying times that all of us experience. An elderly woman who cared for her disabled son twenty-four/seven showed me her bookmark when I visited her to help with complicated Medicaid requirements. Other constituents told me the poem inspired them when fighting a serious illness, seeking employment, studying for important exams or dealing with a child's or their own drug addiction.

Having a large extended family and good friends with several children made canvassing almost every neighborhood possible during all my campaigns. We affectionately described Terrie and Don Craven and their six children as "the landing of paratroopers" as they exited their minivan and quickly delivered brochures to neighborhoods!

Sign-holding standouts (when campaigners literally stand out on the streets and sidewalks to pass out brochures and talk with constituents) and rallies with lots of people holding signs were good for building name recognition and involving local supporters. We scheduled weekly standouts during evening commute times at busy intersections in my three towns. On the weekend before Halloween, we wore costumes while holding signs along Route 18 through all three towns. It was always encouraging to see drivers return my wave and hear cars honk with support. This was a time when respect for others was still valued, even toward politicians in an opposing party. In some campaigns, candidates with a lot of money paid outsiders to knock on doors, collect nomination signatures, and hold signs. We didn't have that option, nor would we have chosen it.

I delivered my policy messages in debates; on cable TV and local radio shows; at coffee hours and house parties; in telephone calls, mailings, and political ads in newspapers; and on my website. Facebook, blogs, and tweets were not yet popular. As I had learned from my first campaign, it was vitally important to be able to define myself and my stands on the issues, while not allowing my opponent to define me. Professional campaign managers present their candidates in favorable ways and often define opponents in negative ways. During my first two campaigns, Republican brochures contained sensational words like "scheme," "disguised contribution," "outrage," "special break," and "windfall," to create an unfavorable and dishonest image of me. It seemed to be Standard operating procedure (SOP).

Political experts research the positive images that will resonate favorably with voters in a certain place at a certain time. During my former House colleague Scott Brown's campaign for a Massachusetts U.S. Senate seat and later a New Hampshire Senate seat, he used a pickup truck and wore a barn jacket suggesting physical labor and a close connection with the working class. I know other politicians who kept an old car to use for campaigns, so they'd come across as a member of the blue-collar working class.

"Push polls" (a technique of using questions under the guise

End The Tax Junkies' 43 Million Dollar A Day Habit.

Kathy Teahan and other tax addicts have fought to increase our tax burden. That's why our state spends over *forty-three million* dollars every day of the year. Our dollars.

Self servingly, she has vigorously opposed Proposition 2 1/2. Money, not education, is what motivates her ally, the MTA teachers' union.

She opposes the construction of new prisons today while favoring more social welfare programs as the solution to crime.

Kathy Teahan opposes cutting the state's public payroll and opposes any effort to streamline state services which would reduce spending.

She opposes the Governor's programs to get welfare under control and off the backs of decent, hard-working families.

As a political pawn of the big government Beacon Hill bosses, Kathy Teahan only knows a future where the state does more and more, spends more and more, and taxes us more and more.

But we know that's not a future. That's the past. The past that cost us jobs, cost our children the ability to buy a home of their own, and cost us a secure life.

We cannot turn the clock back. We need to stop the tax habit now.

Negative campaign brochure used against Kathy by Republican opponent

of a survey on an issue to alter voters' views of a political opponent) were and are another campaign tool. They may include language that insinuates half-truths and are especially effective when done at the end of a campaign when opponents don't learn about them in time to refute them. In push polls used against me, my opponent's campaign workers made telephone calls in the last few days of the campaign, asking voters a hot-button question about supporting me when I "sided with murderers rather than victims" because of my stand against the death penalty.

Campaigns are all about people

What I learned from my six campaigns (the special election that I lost in 1995 and five other legislative elections that occur every other year) is that voters want representatives who will listen to their needs and ideas, who will be honest with them, and who will not duck their questions but answer them in clear and straight-forward statements. They want people they elect to have the interests of the people they represent as their first priority, not the special interests of those who contribute generously to their campaigns.

I also learned that you don't win elections by yourself. I had wonderful people who answered my call for help or volunteered to work on my campaigns. My parents, siblings, aunts, uncles, and children gave endless hours of support. As my campaign treasurer, my sister Eileen had to adhere to the Massachusetts Office of Campaign and Political Finance's strict accounting regulations for all donations and expenditures. During one campaign, we sold some 200 Teahan buttons for one dollar each and because the donations totaled more than fifty dollars, we had to report the names of every person who had purchased a button!!

For each campaign, Kay and Charlie Pagnini, and later Linda Uftring (all three first-time campaign volunteers who stuck with me throughout my legislative career), ran our Democratic headquarters like tight ships. (They also served the best soup on cold Election

Days!) They efficiently called volunteers to stuff and address envelopes, hold signs before town meetings and Fourth of July fireworks, and serve as vote checkers who sat beside election workers and kept records of my supporters as they voted. We later called supporters who hadn't voted to get them to the polls. These dedicated volunteers were people I knew from church, members of the Democratic Town Committees, teachers and former students, and strangers who walked into headquarters wanting to help. Some of these volunteers, such as Helen Zak, who has remained positive and active throughout her life, though challenged with vision problems, Michael Celona, who currently serves as Chief of Water Toxics at the Massachusetts Department of Environmental Protection, and Jennifer Oriola, who worked several years as a senate legislative aide, became lifelong friends.

As I later mentored interns and helped political newcomers, I became part of the "nuts and bolts" of other candidates' grass-roots campaigns. And I will always remember with gratitude and love the hundreds of volunteers who gave of themselves in many ways to serve as the "nuts" and "bolts" and "Sledges" and "Stakes" in my own campaigns.

Chapter 3: Nomination Papers
(aka Collecting Signatures and Life Stories)

In my six campaigns, I always began by gathering nomination signatures from my family members who lived in the district and from my Harvard Street neighbors. Every signature represented an individual, his or her family, and lots of hopes and dreams for a decent life.

In 1995, Whitman was a mostly blue-collar community. We weren't a wealthy community materially; we were a community of citizens who knew each other and contributed to the well-being of all, which made it a wonderful place to live. Whitman is about six square miles surrounding a town center. There, all within walking distance, you would find: two white wooden Protestant churches with large clocks and spires (one of these churches was sold and has been converted into condominiums); a large brown Roman Catholic church that was an important part of my life; a classic 1907 brick town hall; a granite War Memorial Arch; a brick fire station; three banks; Duval's Pharmacy; Menard's Jewelers; several pizza places and breakfast/lunch spots, and coffee shops; the Clothes Clinic Cleaner; a dental office; three car-repair shops; three hair salons; a nail salon; two dance studios; a gift shop; and a Family Dollar Store (previously home to Joubert's Clothing Store). It was a fairly typical New England town. In December s until about twenty years ago, Christmas lights hung across the center of town as they do in the movie, *It's a Wonderful Life*.

Located behind the town hall are the Whitman Town Park, designed by Frederick Law Olmsted landscape designers, and a busy senior citizen center. At the other end of the park, diagonally across from it, is the new police station. Just beyond the center are two large buildings that once housed bustling shoe factories; now they are condominiums and apartment complexes.

When I was growing up in the 1950s, the Commonwealth Shoe Factory, which was famous for its Bostonian men's shoes, employed hundreds of area residents. In the center of town were Sally's Dress Shop; Dorothy Ann's children and women's clothing store; Joubert's Shoe Store; Rosen's Furniture Store; the Whitman Shop; Buckley's Taxi Stand; two markets (Cavicchi's and Bucken's); the First National Grocery; Freeman's Hardware; Vaughan (my Uncle Sewall Vaughan) and Benson TV; Fossila's Tailor Shop; barber shops; hair salons; a busy Five and Ten Cents department store; and the G.A.R (Grand Army of the Republic) Hall. Whitman was and still is a great place to raise a family. When you're walking through this small town, people are friendly. They support great schools and youth athletic programs; and they help neighbors in need and do a lot for those less fortunate. For most of my life, Whitman was a very "white" community because before the 1970s, realtors didn't show available homes to Black families.

Beginning each campaign on Harvard Street was like being in a microcosm of my district and it motivated me for all the hard work that was to follow. I remember vividly, during my first campaign (1995), gathering nomination signatures from my neighbors and visiting an elderly widower who lived in a studio apartment at 65 Harvard Street, right across the street from us. A couple days after I had knocked on his door, he called me. He was crying and seemed depressed as he told me about his loneliness after losing his wife and moving into this small apartment. I scheduled an appointment for him with Eleanor Canty, who was the very competent and caring assistant director at our local Housing Authority. The man qualified for emergency status and soon moved into senior housing where he met new friends and became much happier.

I also got signatures from parents who were scoutmasters in their children's Boy and Girl Scout troops. I later spoke and answered questions at troop meetings to help young boys and girls earn their civics badges; and after I was elected, I was happy to host their field trips and show them around the State House.

Mrs. Thrasher, a sweet woman who lived six houses down from us, signed my papers. Mrs. Thrasher was a widow in her late 70s. She had health problems of her own but was the caregiver for her sixteen-year-old, severely disabled granddaughter who could not walk, talk, or feed herself and could not use the toilet. Mrs. Thrasher pushed Nicole's wheelchair up and down Harvard Street whenever the weather permitted. (When Mrs. T. became too weak to lift Nicole into bed at night, my son John would do the lifting for her, and we became good friends.)

Jim Thorndike, a young, hard-working small business owner, signed my papers. June Millet, my former math teacher who made sandwiches on Sundays for people at the homeless shelter in Brockton and opened her large home to women who needed assistance after surgery, a divorce, or other problems, signed my papers.

My former science teacher, David Campbell, and his wife Mary, generous "tippers" on my son John's paper route, signed my papers. Lena Marchetti, my former CYO chaperone who volunteered at the church thrift store, signed my papers. A young mother who offered daycare in her home signed my papers. Eleanor Canty, the SHINE (Serving the Health and Insurance Needs of Elders) volunteer who helped hundreds of our elderly with health and housing questions, signed my papers.

My neighbor Bill Brine, who had become disabled and lived with much pain after a serious car accident, signed my papers. Bill and I had long talks about how his faith helped him deal with his challenges. One night early in my political career, I was alone in a Town Hall office being yelled at by an extremely disgruntled constituent. He was right in my face telling me what was wrong with Democratic policies. That night Bill came to my office hours at the Town Hall just to say hello. His timely visit gave me a graceful way to end that very uncomfortable situation. Blanche Kuzborski lived beside the Brines. Her late husband "Ikey" had been a very popular custodian at the Frank E. Holt Elementary School. Blanche always invited me in for a cup of tea or at least a chat.

A newly married couple who had recently moved to Harvard Street signed my papers, and then brought me to see ducklings swimming in the brook behind their house. The Early sisters, two well-educated elderly women, always invited me in for a lively chat about international and national politics and always signed my papers. Lori Toomey was a neighbor who chaired the Holt School Fun Fair every year, was active in the Knights of Columbus with her husband Richard, and was a very skilled organizer and secretary. She signed my papers, and volunteered to help with my campaign.

My good Republican friend across the street, Bob Dyer, couldn't sign my papers, but he put my campaign signs on his lawn. He was a Braintree firefighter who was always willing to give neighbors a helping hand. One cold, wintery night, Bob rescued our golden retriever, Honey, when she became lodged under our deck. Likewise, I helped round up the Dyer's golden retriever whenever he escaped. (I even petted the pet rat and all the toads and snakes the Dyer children collected.)

Clearly, there was a lot more to nomination papers than gathering signatures. As the years went by, all the people in my district became neighbors to me, and I got to know many of them very well. I believe, as a very wise and caring minister expressed, "It's a representative's responsibility to know the names and circumstances of the people he/she serves." (See Appendix 4 for more information about gathering signatures on nomination papers.)

Chapter 4: Legislative Aides and Interns—From Public Servants to Lifelong Friends

The first chapter of the 1780 Massachusetts Constitution, the oldest written constitution still in effect in the world, gives the Massachusetts Legislature or General Court its powers. The Massachusetts General Court consists of two branches: the House of Representatives (160 members) and the Senate (40 members), each of which functions by its own set of rules.

At the beginning of each legislative session, upon being elected by the members as speaker of the house or senate president, he/she proposes new rules or changes to existing rules. Members vote to accept or protest these rules. A dissenting vote is considered a vote of no-confidence in the leadership of the speaker or senate president! The House Rules state that each representative would have one legislative aide, and the speaker of the house could determine if a legislative office warranted additional aides. From what I experienced, loyalty to the speaker generally determined how many aides a representative was allotted. The two speakers, Thomas Finneran and Sal DiMasi, under whose leadership I served, allotted me only one aide.

A delicate, critical choice

Choosing the right legislative aide was and continues to be critical. Legislative aides are the voice and face of the representatives. They answer the phone, greet visitors, and keep the office organized. They are also the representative's extra eyes and ears, attending meetings and functions at the State House, in the district, and in other locations where issues important to the district or legislation are being discussed. Sometimes aides are asked to say a few words on behalf of their legislators. In the office, they work hand-in-hand with the representative or senator on submissions for the annual budget; writing and advocating for legislation; helping draft letters, press releases, speeches; and helping with constituent requests, as well as many other special projects. A representative must have total trust and confidence that his/her aide is treating people with respect, maintaining the confidentiality of constituent matters, keeping up with tasks, and being loyal.

I thought very carefully before I chose my first legislative aide. Some of the suggestions I received from two female Brockton reps were: one of my Democratic opponents; a State House "insider" whom the Speaker might recommend; a loyal Democrat from the district; or possibly a recent political science graduate who might be a good choice. I brainstormed lists of potential aides and one by one eliminated each one. The characteristics I sought were compassion and kindness, in addition to loyalty, education, skills, and competency.

It was less than a month before I was to take the oath of office, and I was getting anxious about my lack of an aide. Finally, Edna Donoghue's name popped into my head. Edna's daughter Mary had been a student in my English class at the East Bridgewater Middle School. Like me, Edna had been an English teacher and a religious education coordinator. She had helped on my campaign, and she was out of work. I called her, and within twenty-four hours, she had taken the job. Neither of us knew exactly what we were getting into!

Working in downtown Boston after my years in our small South Shore towns was quite a change. Standing in front of an elevator during my first visit to the State House was traumatic: I couldn't even find the "up" and "down" buttons! They were two bronze protrusions, one above the other, without labels. Using telephones with a "hold" option was another challenge. We lost a few calls and cried a few tears. Edna and I drove to Boston together four days a week for four years, shared the legislative responsibilities, confided the challenges of our families, our faith, and life in general, and became best of friends. On September 12, 1997, the day my husband suddenly died, Edna's husband Leo was preparing for surgery to remove a cancerous kidney. As soon as Leo was out of surgery, Edna was at my house with love and support for my family and me. (Thank goodness, Leo's surgery was a success, and he has been living with his remaining healthy kidney ever since.)

The following year (1998), while Edna's daughter Mary was studying at Boston University, Edna was offered a position at the university that would have included the free tuition benefit allotted to employee family members. Edna declined the offer and stayed with me for my first four years in the legislature, earning just under $30,000 a year, not enough to pay even one year of Mary's tuition!

At the end of 2000, Edna was preparing to take a job at the American Cancer Society, and I was in a quandary about her replacement. Out of the clear blue sky, Jennifer Lynch, a former student from the Gordon Mitchell Middle School, called me. Jen had been one of those especially wonderful students in my class; our personalities "clicked," and we had stayed in touch after her middle school years. She had spent a summer in my legislative office as my first intern through the Massachusetts Senate Legislative Office Intern Program. She called to let me know she had graduated from the University of Massachusetts with degrees in microbiology, Spanish, and teaching. Although she had a potential position at the Massachusetts Department of Public Health, she didn't feel quite right about it. I offered Jen the aide job and obtained my second perfect professional staffer!

Constituent David Phillips, Kathy, and Jennifer (Lynch) Horton, Legislative Aide

As a former intern, Jen already knew the office procedures. As a person who had considered a career in medicine, she was very interested in public health policy, which was the focus of my legislative activities. As a person with a very organized, analytical, photographic memory, Jen enabled me to keep up with the ever increasing workload. Foremost, as Edna had, Jen cared about people.

After almost four years as my aide and right hand, Jen completed her master's degree in public health, and it was time for her to move on. She accepted a position in the State Department of Public Health working on the National Comprehensive Cancer Control Program as coordinator of their colorectal cancer segment. She gathered data in collaboration with the entire cancer continuum, from research and prevention through palliative care and end of life, to develop the "Massachusetts Dialogue for Action." This information provided evidence for planning appropriate and sustainable cancer prevention and treatment policies and systems in Massachusetts. Like so many others I met while working in the public sector, Jen was dedicated as well as highly qualified to work on matters concerning the common good. We remain in contact, mostly by

One of my fondest "Jennifer moments" involved a homeless sixty-plus-year-old woman who had been wandering around the State House looking for help. Maybe she was hoping to spend the night there? This woman was very intelligent, had come from a well-to-do family, was almost totally deaf, and had mental health problems. Like many homeless people, she spent her monthly Social Security disability checks on a boarding house or motel room until the money ran out, and by the end of the month, she was back on the streets until the following month. Jen brought her to our office. We spent hours getting her food, writing (the only way to "speak" to her through her deafness) whatever we needed to communicate to her and making arrangements for a bed for her at Fr. Bill's Homeless Shelter in Quincy. We drove her to Fr. Bill's, made sure someone there was taking care of her, and went home.

email these days because Jen is busy with her four children, and I'm busy with my family and grandchildren. We try to meet once a year for breakfast or lunch and to catch up, since we value our continued friendship.

My third legislative aide, Michael Power, was yet another person who was just what I needed as an aide. Beginning in my first term as a legislator, I had received notes from "Irish" Mary Power, an elderly resident at the Sachem Skilled Nursing Home in East Bridge-water. Mary would send me newspaper clippings that mentioned me and the events I attended, poems and prayers that she wrote, and in-spirational thoughts and verses. She also invited me to visit her at the nursing home, and I did visit a couple of times. She often spoke of her life in Ireland and how she made a new life in the United States. Mary had owned a small neighborhood store and shared a home with her son John, his wife Carol, and their two sons until her early 90s when her health deteriorated. Michael was Mary's younger grandson. When I was teaching at the East Bridgewater Middle School, I got to know Carol, as a wonderful teachers' aide, and Michael, as a very popular student.

During my re-election campaign in 2002, Michael Power signed on as a very active campaign volunteer. Mike was a dedicated campaigner; he had a fun and spirit-filled personality, was interested in government, and he loved people. As Jen Lynch (now Jen Horton) was leaving my office, I asked Mike for suggestions for my next aide. He said that he'd love a shot at it, and I was blessed to have Mike at my side for the last two and a half years of my legislative career. Because of his charismatic personality and his dedication to good government, Anne Ziaja, who was the executive director for the Sen-ate Legislative Education Office and ran the Senate Intern Program, had Mike speak to our interns every summer.

Mike never said "no" to my many requests for help that often required endless hours beyond the legislative workday. He never once complained about late hours we spent at the State House during budget week or when we were trying to get through the piles of constituent requests. He even endured the wrath of a local parish priest who called the office to complain about my stand on requiring public reporting of church finances in the same way that all other charities reported theirs. The priest yelled at Mike, who was not the person who had taken this stand, telling him that neither he nor I would be welcome at any parish events except to receive the sacraments.

Choosing the right legislative aides was, for me, a win-win situation. My aides all became friends I continue to cherish, and we supported each other as we helped hundreds of people in our district of Abington, East Bridgewater and Whitman.

Ironically, it was a legislative aide issue that later caused me to leave the legislature in 2007.

Chapter 5: Too Nice for Politics?

After I lost the 1995 special election for State Representative for the 7th Plymouth District, my eighty-year-old friend Ellen Callanan invited me to her home and offered me some advice. In 1960 Ellen and her husband Joe, both lifelong Democrats, had moved from Boston to my hometown of Whitman, a six-square-mile town twenty-six miles south of Boston. There weren't many Democrats in Whitman at that time, but Ellen and Joe worked tirelessly for Democratic candidates. Sitting in her living room on Homeland Drive, Ellen said, "Some people didn't vote for you because you are too nice. They feel you won't survive in the tough world of politics. If you're going to win this next election, you've got to show them that you're tough!"

Ellen wasn't the only one offering that advice. Other campaign volunteers were telling me pretty much the same thing. They were a very experienced group that included my husband Bob, who had been a state representative in the 1970s, other former legislators (Jack Buckley of Abington, Robert McCarthy of East Bridgewater, Emmet Hayes of Whitman), town officials, and many political activists. They all wanted me to "go negative" in my next campaign to prove my toughness.

Rejecting negative campaigning

In that second attempt in 1996, I would again be running against my former student and, now-Representative Ronald Whitney, who had beaten me by just seventy-five votes in the special election. His success in that race seemed to depend on negative campaign tactics. Much of his campaign literature was modeled after the negative tactics used in Newt Gingrich's Republican campaign playbook. Brochures the Republicans distributed included "canned" phrases about unpopular, hot-button issues and created a negative image of me for voters in my conservative district. Descriptions of me as a teacher wanting to "continue feeding off the public trough," and as someone connected to Billy Bulger—the very powerful Democratic senate president and brother of notorious South Boston gangster Whitey Bulger—implied that I was a political hack. I totally rejected both descriptions.

As a teacher, I had hardly been "feeding off the public trough," often spending my own money on books, supplies, and other items for my classes because our budgets did not supply them; and I had never even met Senator Bulger prior to my election. Whitney's campaign materials also, by innuendo, associated my support from the Massachusetts Teachers Association with being in favor of raising taxes and handing out condoms in public schools. His campaign committee used last minute "push-poll" calls and mailings that didn't leave me any time for rebuttals.

I didn't want to get into a negative campaign. I had grown up on the same street as my opponent's wife; and I was a Eucharistic Minister at Holy Ghost Church where his own son served as an altar boy. As a middle-school teacher, I had taught my students about integrity, social responsibility, and the importance of each voter's careful consideration of the candidates' positions on issues. Even after my loss, I still wanted to show my students and others that it was possible to achieve a political victory without resorting to mudslinging. How was I going to do that?

Early in the second campaign (March 1996), I was driving to the Barnside Restaurant on Route 53 in Hanover to meet a group of high school girlfriends for our annual luncheon, and I was surfing the radio stations for a good talk show. I happened to catch a program discussing whether Christians who wanted to bring about peace and justice could justify confrontation and conflict. The answer, as the conclusion went, was that while Jesus was loving and kind, he was certainly no doormat. That was it!!! I would campaign positively and honestly. However, I was also determined not to let my opponent define me or my stands on issues. I would tell voters outright about my opponent's activities that might not be in their best interests. From that day on, when necessary, in debates, printed campaign literature, or door-to-door discussions, I presented what I believed my opponent was doing that did not benefit the district. In the process, I supported my accusations with proper references, citing dates and places as sources for my information.

The '96 campaign was grueling: knocking on doors in sweltering heat, holding signs from 6:30 to 8 a.m. during the early morning commute and again during the supper-time commute. My volunteers and I worked late into the night on campaign literature. I helped raise money to fund the campaign, attended civic events and special interest group meetings, and debated my opponents. A third candidate, Libertarian Steve Olson, was also running in this race. In the end, I won this, my second, campaign by more than 1,200 votes. Tenacity, clarity, and niceness were not mutually exclusive!

Devoting energy to children's oral health

In 1998, during my second budget session in the House of Representatives, I dedicated myself to improving the oral health of Massachusetts children.

I had learned that the most common childhood disease, dental disease, could be prevented. Poor oral health could compromise the health of people who had heart disease, diabetes, and other chronic conditions, and I learned it could also cause premature births. Eighty percent of dental decay could be prevented through routine checkups, cleanings, and sealants. The political will to fund these inexpensive measures for adults as well as children would have prevented pain, embarrassing tooth loss, and loss of money.

Yet, MassHealth for adults and the Children's Medical Security Program (CHIP), government-subsidized insurance plans for low-income families, didn't cover dental care. MassHealth for Children included oral health coverage, but payments to dentists were so low, there was a scarcity of available dentists. With the help of Allison Staton, who was an energetic and knowledgeable children's health advocate, and a non-profit group, Health Care for All, I drafted and submitted an amendment to the FY99 budget that would expand these two programs for children's dental health. I talked to nearly all of my 160 House colleagues about this budget amendment, and ninety-two members eventually signed onto it, eleven more than the eighty-one votes needed to create a majority and pass an amendment.

Around midnight during a late-night budget session, my amendment came up for debate. I was nervous but ready. My heart was pounding, and my palms were sweaty as I stood up in the Chamber and asked the speaker to be recognized. He must have been surprised because he gaveled the session to a brief recess and called me up to the rostrum. Even when I told him about the support I had for my amendment, he said I needed to talk with the Ways and Means staff to understand why the House should not accept the amendment. As the young Ways and Means staffers showed me numbers and talked about issues they had with the administration of the two children's health programs, the needs of low-income Massachusetts children remained firmly stuck in my mind. In the end, the staffers did not persuade me to remove my amendment. Then, after another ten difficult minutes of arguing the case for my amendment quietly but nose to nose with Speaker Finneran, the Speaker called Representative Harriette Chandler, the chair of the Public Health Committee, to the rostrum.

The chairwoman, who I wholeheartedly respected, talked with me for about twenty minutes about the Speaker's concerns with my amendment. I finally withdrew my amendment, but on the condition that the Speaker would personally look at this issue in the near future. (He eventually supported some of my oral-health amendments, but it was, to me and the children, much longer than the "near future.") I also withdrew it because, as a first-term rep, I didn't want to "spot" my colleagues.(You "spotted" members by forcing them to take a vote against the Speaker's position. You see, when the Speaker of the House didn't want a bill or amendment to pass, he expected loyalty from his caucus members, which meant voting the same way he voted. If I had asked for a vote on my amendment, my colleagues voting "yay" risked losing favor with the Speaker, whom—as it will become clear—had a tight control over legislative activities. If they voted "nay," they risked losing favor with constituents.)

The session continued, and I returned to my seat, with applause from my colleagues for holding up the session to argue with the Speaker. This would not be the last time I stood up to the leadership.

In 1999, two years had passed since the horrific murder of ten-year-old Jeffrey Curley. (On October 1, 1997, at approximately 3:15 in the afternoon, Jeffrey was lured into a car and murdered that afternoon by two men, one who had been working in his Cambridge neighborhood.) Then Governor Paul Cellucci, who supported the death penalty, was standing near the grand staircase in the State House speaking to reporters about his goal to reinstate the death penalty in Massachusetts. I heard the Governor mention that the death penalty could discourage such murders. In all my campaign research on the death penalty, I had learned that most murders occurred in moments of passion, rage, and panic, and that the death penalty did not provide a deterrent. Standing beside a reporter, I interrupted the interview and spoke about that research. Two days later, I called Governor Cellucci to apologize for interrupting his conversation. He was very kind and told me it was never wrong to stand up for what I strongly believed.

For the people: against the Speaker

Around 11 p.m. during another late-night budget session—this time the FY2003 budget—I took the floor to ask my colleagues to vote against an Outside Section of the budget (see Appendix 5) that would place a $1.30 surcharge on every prescription filled in Mass-achusetts. The 2003 House budget had 247 Outside Sections that year. (Outside Sections are ways to explain in more detail how appropriations in line items will be distributed. Sometimes, as in this case, they hide controversial legislation.) This surcharge on people who were ill would go toward paying our ever increasing state Medicaid expenses. I had made an amendment to eliminate this surcharge from the budget. I knew the pharmaceutical companies received enormously profitable state and federal contracts and that they could well afford to give the state a better bulk-purchasing price for prescriptions. These were the savings that could help us pay for Medicaid programs for the poor and disabled! But because the Speaker opposed my amendment, only a handful of Democrats joined the Republicans and me in voting for it, and, unfortunately, the pharmacy tax passed.

But soon after this tax surcharge went into effect, a maelstrom of public anger pressured the Legislature to reverse its support for it. My budget amendment removing the surcharge on prescriptions alerted my colleagues about the ramifications of taxing the ill to fund health care for the poor—I had tried to help my colleagues as well as our constituents. If they had followed my lead and voted against the Speaker, we could have saved our constituents and ourselves the time and energy it required to finally reverse this surcharge on prescriptions.

Against the death penalty and war

On September 12, 2001, while the nation was in shock after the previous day's attacks on the World Trade Center and the Pentagon, I was speaking to the senior class at my alma mater, Whitman-Hanson Regional High School. My visit had been previously scheduled for the annual Legislators Back to School Day, sponsored by the Council on State Governments, to encourage civic involvement among young adults. The first questions the students asked me were: Would I support the death penalty for anyone we found guilty of the 9/11 attacks? And would I support a war against the people who were behind the attacks? (My talk was being taped by the students for possible airing on our local cable channel.)

My stand on the death penalty was a tough one to explain to the students that day, at a time when people's emotions were so raw from the images of the collapsing towers, exploding planes, and the deaths of so many innocent Americans. Nevertheless, my stance still stood. No, I would not support the death penalty for the 9/11 perpetrators, I told them, because I felt it would not be a deterrent. It was unfairly administered (predominantly to minorities and those who could not afford skilled lawyers) and it promoted and perpetuated violence. No one voiced opposition to my opinions. I think all of us were still in shock

I hadn't expected to be asked about my stand on war.

I told the students that I believed too many young and innocent people died in wars and a war against terrorism would fuel more extremists to perform more acts of terrorism. I didn't know enough about our national security or whether we needed to go to war to defend ourselves. But I asked for a show of hands about supporting a war, and at least ninety-five percent of the students were in favor of war against the terrorists. I skirted the question and suggested the students watch the movie *Saving Private Ryan* as a way of considering how they would feel about being drafted, or having family members drafted, to fight in a war, and I urged them to learn more about wars before deciding that war was a solution to terrorism. (Bob, a WW II Veteran, had fought in the Battle of the Bulge, as depicted in this movie, and September 12, 2001, was the third anniversary of Bob's death.)

Even though I still believe war creates more problems than it solves and sacrifices too many innocent lives, just twenty-four hours after the 9/11 attack, I wasn't prepared to give the students a yes or no answer. In retrospect, especially as the U. S. attacked Iraq, I wished I had expressed my views against war more definitively to the students that day! Unfortunately, after the September 11 terrorist attacks, any views that differed from the American pro-war majority were considered unpatriotic. We fought a preemptive war in Iraq when there were no weapons of mass destruction, and most of the world disagreed with our attacks there. Some 6800 Americans lost their lives in Iraq and Afghanistan, and at least 55,000 suffered serious physical injuries. And who knows how many lost their mental equilibrium to nightmares and flashbacks due to post traumatic stress disorder (PTSD)? An estimated 200,000-plus combined Iraqi and Afghan civilians and combatants died during that war. How many of their family members now detest Americans and might become future terrorists?

Opposing the Speaker's support for local improvement districts

A couple of years later, in a 2006 formal session of the House, I spoke in opposition to overriding the governor's veto of Section 41 of the Economic Stimulus Bill that would have created Chapter 40T under the General Laws of Massachusetts. Section 41 would enable developers and large landowners to create their own governmental entities called "local improvement districts" (LIDs) within exist- ing municipalities. It would give developers the power to issue tax-exempt bonds and levy assessments (property taxes) to pay for their "infrastructure," which when broadly defined included parking garages, recreation and cultural facilities, and other profitable im- provements.

These new governments-within-governments would be exempt from many public-interest safeguards, including public records law, oversight by the Massachusetts Department of Revenue, and laws governing public construction, civil service, conflicts of interest, and more. I stated my opinion that the bill would benefit special-interest private developers more than it would benefit the people of Massa- chusetts. Speaker Sal DiMasi strongly supported Chapter 40T and so did most of his leadership team. When I returned to my seat, one of my younger male colleagues tapped me on the back and said, "Kathy, you've got balls!" (I still think it's both courageous and nice to oppose legislation that benefits a chosen few on the backs of unknowing citizens.) The House did pass the override, but the Senate did not take it up. (I was extremely happy that we had two branches of the legislature!)

Nice, and tough?

In December 2006, House members who were leaving the legislature made farewell speeches to colleagues. A member of my legislative Class of '97, Rep. Tom O'Brien (D-Halifax), as part of his farewell, gave out O-B (short for O'Brien) Awards, his version of the Academy Awards. He presented me with the "Nicest Democrat" Award. When I see today's lack of civility in Congress, and I hear debates that are more about getting re-elected than about finding common ground for compromises for the general good, I think "nice" may not be such a bad quality for a politician!

Chapter 6: From Cookie to the Tooth Fairy

Every day of my ten years in the Massachusetts Legislature was an exciting, energizing, and often challenging adventure. The nicknames "Cookie" and "Tooth Fairy," given to me by my male colleagues, stand as the bookends for what was truly a ten-year journey. During my first term in the legislature, Representative Bob Hargraves (R-Groton), and several other reps began to call me "Cookie." This is how I got the nickname.

The Chocolate Chip Cookie Bill

It began with a bill filed by Senator Thomas (D-Fall River) and Representative Joan Menard (D-Somerset) to make the Toll House chocolate chip cookie the official Massachusetts state cookie.

Third graders from the Chace Elementary School in Somerset had recently completed an interdisciplinary learning project centered on a cookie theme. First the students took a poll to determine the most popular cookie in their school, and the Toll House chocolate chip cookie—the 1930 creation of Ruth Wakefield, owner of the Toll House Restaurant in Whitman—beat the oatmeal raisin, pea-nut butter, and sugar cookies hands down! As the math part of the unit, students made charts and graphs showing the results of their poll. Next, they took out a loan to buy the ingredients and supplies needed to bake and sell Toll House cookies. They then had to figure what to charge for each cookie in order to make a profit, which they later voted to donate to the Somerset food pantry. Students baked the cookies and then made posters, wrote advertising jingles, and sold the cookies in the school cafeteria. During a visit to the Chace Elementary School, Senator Norton challenged these third graders to petition the Massachusetts Legislature to make chocolate chip cook-ies the official state cookie of Massachusetts. In the past, teachers throughout Massachusetts had had their classes lobby to make the ladybug our state bug, the cranberry our state berry, the Boston terrier our state dog, as a hands-on way to learn the legislative process.

When Senator Norton asked me to be the lead sponsor in the House for the cookie bill, I was happy to support the Somerset students in this excellent project. All present and former residents of Whitman, including me, were very proud of this cookie and the Toll House Restaurant where it had been invented. Ernie Pyle, the beloved World War II journalist, had written three syndicated columns about the Toll House Restaurant after his visit there in 1938. In his columns, Pyle had praised Toll House owners Ruth and Ken Wakefield for their perseverance during the Great Depression and the consistent quality their customers enjoyed. My three aunts had waitressed at the Toll House in its early years, and I had been a salad girl there the summer before my senior year of college. After Whitman lost most of its industries in the 1960s, the Toll House chocolate chip cookie was the town's claim to fame. These delicious confections were part of our culture and had been baked by friends and loved ones and even packaged and sent to American military forces overseas since World War II. So, of course I co-sponsored the bill. There was a lot of support from my district for the bill, although I didn't want my constituents to get the wrong message: that my first term's accomplishment was successful passage of a cookie bill!

Toll House vs. Fig Newton

But as it happened, there was competition! The press gave a lot of attention to our cookie bill, and also to Governor William Weld's preference for the Fig Newton as our state cookie. Representative Peter Koutoujian's Newton constituents, after hearing about the Toll House cookie bill, pressured Koutoujian to push the Fig Newton for status as the official cookie. As the legislature debated an annual budget of over $20 billion, and I sent out press releases about local aid and health care items I fought for in the budget, all the newspapers, radio, and even TV wanted to hear about was the cookie debate. Even from as far away as Great Britain, a news reporter from the British

Broadcasting Company (BBC) called and said, "We hear you're debating biscuits over there in Massachusetts!" Peter Koutoujian and I were on WGBH/TV for a segment about our cookie debate. I still have a scrapbook called, "From the Toll House to the State House," full of press clippings from the great cookie debate. Thankfully, we never actually debated the cookie bill in a formal session.

Meanwhile, the House and Senate passed the bill during informal sessions, and on July 10, 1997, Governor Weld signed the bill into law, flanked by platters of Toll House cookies that were later distributed to State House visitors. Whitman celebrated our cookie's historical recognition with a Toll House Cookie Day, which included a small parade, the sale of homemade Toll House cookies to raise $1,000 for our food pantry, a reunion of Toll House workers, a $25,000 donation from the Nestle Food Company for new playground equipment in the Whitman Park, and satisfied constituents. (Nestle created the first chocolate chips just for Toll House cookies more than eighty-four years ago.) A few years after passage of the cookie bill, Nestle gave an additional $25,000 to further renovate the Whitman Town Park. (Cookies or not, this was the sort of thing that delighted constituents and brought them together with their state government.)

Benefits of the informal session

The informal legislative session passing the cookie bill was appropriate, as were the informal passages of hundreds of bills that recognized achievements: Eagle Scout Awards, retirements of public officials, and hundredth birthdays. Informal sessions were and continue to be a way to take care of home-rule petitions, such as locally-voted changes to town charters and other non-controversial bills. Without informal sessions, the House would not have had the time to act on all bills that came before it, even if it stayed in session for forty hours a week, 365 days a year. The informal session actually protected me from critical media coverage about my first-term efforts to pass a bill about a cookie. Things happen so fast and quietly in informal sessions that reporters don't usually pay close attention to them. Often only a dozen or so legislators participated during informal sessions, which occurred more often than the formal sessions in which the entire House of Representatives participated. This is still the case.

While very time consuming, it is important to know what happens in the informal sessions because during these sessions House or Senate rules are suspended to allow bills to move forward without going through the usual process or required oversight. Also, without members' knowledge, changes may be made to a bill on the docket before it is passed during an informal session. Sometimes informal sessions are used to pass controversial legislation. When I was available, I would help a group of progressive legislators keep an eye and ear on informal sessions. (Disclaimer: I voted to suspend the rules during a few of these sessions.) (Look for more about informal sessions and suspension of rules in Appendix 6.)

Going on-site to learn

With the Toll House Cookie Bill signed into law in July 1997, I spent the rest of my legislative time that year on extremely serious issues and sometimes visited sites around the state to learn more about these issues. As a way to gain my support for the Perfusionist Licensure Bill, New England Medical Center invited me to their cardiac department operating room to watch a perfusionist operate a machine that kept blood flowing through the patient's body during open heart surgery.

Seeing a technician with specialized training and skills perform this life-sustaining function quickly secured my support of a bill to license perfusionists. My intern at the time was planning to go to medical school so I asked if he could come along. (He watched the entire surgery, although for me the exposed beating heart, blood, and other body parts made me dizzy and shortened my visit.)

Because I was a member of the Joint Committee on Public Health, I visited several community hospitals as well as several of the larger city hospitals, including Mass General, Dana-Faber (now

Dana-Faber/Brigham and Women's Cancer Institute), and Boston Children's Hospital. Hospital issues ranged from physician credentialing, hospital closings, the use of robotics in surgery, safe nurse staffing, insurance and Medicaid payments to hospitals and nursing facilities, babies born with fetal alcohol syndrome or drug addictions, the threat of exposure to AIDS and Hepatitis C from needles and other sharps, and emergency medical responses for train accidents on newly restored rail lines and for terrorist attacks after 9/11.

During the SARS outbreak in 2003, we were receiving information from the National Centers for Disease Control (CDC) about possible SARS cases in the U.S. The CDC had activated its Emergency Operations Center to provide round-the-clock coordination and responses to outbreaks. Our own Joint Committee on Public Health held hearings on bills to provide support for preparedness for these outbreaks in Massachusetts. As a former Girl Scout and full-time mother, prevention and preparedness always made sense to me as the best way to tackle problems.

As a legislator, I walked behind the concrete walls of several prisons and into the nightmare of prison life. A few constituents spoke to me about their imprisoned family members. One man, who was serving a two-year sentence for being an accomplice to a counterfeiter, had broken a tooth while at Mass Correctional Institute, Bridgewater, and was suffering terribly with the jagged tooth and exposed nerve. Nothing had been done to ease his pain after many requests from his wife, who offered to pay for the dental care. Another family was trying to help their brother, who began serving a life sentence at MCI-Cedar Junction, Walpole, when he was twenty years old. Although he had come from a loving and supportive family, he had gotten into drugs and was an accomplice to murder (he carried the bat that was used for what became a drug-related murder). Even though he was an exemplary inmate, raising money for charitable causes and mentoring young inmates, each parole attempt he made was denied. My letters and phone calls trying to help these two prisoners were to no avail. I also learned firsthand about a drug-addicted female inmate at a County Correctional Institute who had been left in isolation screaming and vomiting for twenty-four hours a day for nearly a week. It still angers and saddens me that our prisons seem to be more of a way for companies to make money than to protect the public and rehabilitate law-breakers so they can return to society. We need better oversight of the privatization in prisons and other government institutions.

Honoring veterans

As a representative, I was honored and moved to participate in a Congressional Medal of Honor ceremony for Lieutenant John R. Fox from Whitman who was posthumously presented this highest of military medals, fifty years after the end of World War II. John Fox was a Black artillery officer who had sacrificed his life the day after Christmas 1943 in Italy to stop a major enemy advance on his platoon. In 1996 President Clinton presented the Congressional Medal to Fox and six other Black military heroes to finally recognize and thank these individuals for the sacrifices they had made in World War II. Waiting fifty years to recognize people of color who protected us with the same self-sacrificing courage as their White brothers added more pain and suffering for families already grieving the deaths of their sons. Participating in a ceremony at the Whitman VFW to honor Lieutenant Fox was one of the most memorable experiences of my legislative career. Sadly, rather than the prominent place he deserved, Lieutenant Fox was buried in an obscure lot at the rear of Whitman's Colebrook Cemetery.

A few years later, I was honored to be named the Massachusetts team leader for the Library of Congress Veterans Oral History Project. I interviewed several World War II veterans on local cable TV and sent tapes of the interviews to the Library of Congress. The veterans included Clint Jenkins, Harry Blakeman, Edward Sexton, Gene Davidson, William Ulwick, Leslie (Red) Greenleaf, Dan Brundage, George Weir, James Garrison, and Ralph Brett. They were phenomenal individuals who taught me a lot about sacrifice and brotherhood. I wish I had been able to interview, as part of this project, both my deceased father, a World War II Merchant Marine, and my husband Bob, who had fought in Germany at the Battle of the Bulge.

We owe a debt of gratitude to all men and women who serve in our military, and we need to hear from them about the consequences both sides suffer from wars.

The Big Dig and other oversight problems

As a state representative, I descended below the streets of Boston to see slurry poured around the Big Dig tunnel walls. I saw engineering feats that kept Boston traffic moving and skyscrapers standing, while new streets, tunnels, and bridges were constructed right beside, under, and around them.

The Central Artery/Tunnel Project (dubbed "The Big Dig" early on), at a cost of $15 billion plus $9 billion in interest, was the most expensive transportation project in U.S. history (at the time). In Massachusetts, home to MIT, Wentworth Institute of Technology, Worcester Polytechnic Institute, and Harvard, our officials had the resources they needed to do a better job of ensuring the structural and financial integrity of this project. But we still ask, why was it that companies were allowed to ignore safety codes, the advice of structural engineers, and offers of assistance from our great engineering schools? Why wasn't there enough oversight to stop the use of inferior materials that continue to cause safety hazards and other problems? Probably because Bechtel Parsons Brinkerhoff, the company charged with executing the design, was also responsible for monitoring the work as the project manager. In a project of this scope and expense, the project manager should be an objective professional who has the responsibility to review all materials and labor so that the expectations of all stakeholders are met.

In the fall of 2004, a serious wall-joint leak closed the tunnel while it was being sealed. As a consequence, all 9,000 ceiling and wall joints had to be inspected. In addition, there were questions about the quality of the materials involved. During the Central Artery/Tunnel Project, more than $2 billion worth of contract change orders were executed. There should indeed have been more independent oversight of this huge project. Learning the state had awarded this mammoth project to Bechtel for both construction management and oversight seriously reduced my confidence in the integrity of our state government.

Five other female reps and I traveled to Washington, D.C., several times as members of WILL (Women Legislators' Lobby) and WAND (Women's Actions for New Directions) to lobby our Massachusetts congressional delegation about the need for increased oversight of nuclear waste storage and of defense spending, especially the subsidizing of weapons manufacturers through earmarks in the federal budget. Our research showed that more accountability would enable reallocation of wasteful defense dollars to better teach our kids, care for our elderly and disabled, and protect our fragile environment and food supply. In 2010, the United States budgeted $664 billion for defense and $70 billion for K-12 public education. I believed that our budget priorities were out of balance! And they were still out of balance in 2020, with sixteen percent of the federal discretionary budget going to defense and only six percent of discretionary spending slated for public K-12 and higher education.

Fighting for oral health

As a member of the Special Legislative Commission on Oral Health, I joined public health heroes like Myron Allukian, Jr. DDS, MPH, who dedicated his life to improving dental health. During his more than seventy years of service, Dr. Allukian was a leader in his field as dental director for the City of Boston and as president of the American Public Health Association. Repeatedly, Dr. Allukian emphasized that the most cost-effective remedy to children's dental disease is community fluoridation, followed by preventative fluoride rinses, sealants, and regular check-ups. Why was this not happening in one of the richest countries in the world? Our commission was tasked to find the answers.

I drove from one corner of Massachusetts to the other to chair hearings about the need for basic dental care. The Oral Health Crisis in Massachusetts, a report published in 2000, brought together the expertise of oral health professionals, insurance companies, state oral health regulators, public health advocates, community health centers, dental schools, the dental society, and data gathered from my hearings. This report highlighted a major public health need in the state and the country.

During my hearings, I learned that oral health in the state had been neglected and underfunded for decades. School nurses told my colleagues and me about decay in young children's teeth, creating holes that would fit a finger. Because of low government and insurance reimbursements for dental care and the complex reimbursement filing requirements for providers, there was a serious shortage of dentists willing to take on Medicaid patients. Parents waited for weeks and sometimes drove more than a hundred miles for dental appointments for children with toothaches. At the time, there was also a serious lack of Medicaid assistance for adult oral health needs.

Members of our special commission learned that MassHealth had over 4,000 calls a month for dental help, followed by mental health with 700 calls. We learned about research showing dental infection leading to heart problems and strokes as well as complications with diabetes. Infections in pregnant women could cause premature births requiring expensive intensive care for their babies and often long-term special needs services throughout a child's life. Dr. John Hogan and his administrative assistant Cathy Dolan from the Tufts Dental Program for the Developmentally Disabled showed us how their special equipment and training provided oral health care for patients who could not be cared for in a typical dental office. During work on the 2002 state budget, I learned this program, a national model, was in danger of closing some clinics because of funding cuts. We fought hard, and the funding was retained.

My participation in the Special Legislative Commission on Oral Health and our report laid the groundwork for the 2003 adult MassHealth coverage of dental diagnostic exams, preventative cleanings, and restorative fillings. While progress on access to oral health in Massachusetts was very slow during my ten years in the legislature, our work yielded additional improvements to oral health care in 2007 and 2008 after my departure from the legislature. For details about these improvements to oral health care, see the MassHealth Policy Report "Putting the Mouth Back in the Body," in Appendix 7. For a recent resource on the status of oral health in the U.S., see Appendix 8.

Perseverance and my desire for all people to enjoy good health are what motivated my long days of hard work in the legislature. After those many years of working to improve the dental health of Massachusetts residents and my position co-chairing, with Senator Harriette Chandler, the first dental caucus in the country, my fellow legislators changed my nickname to "Tooth Fairy," and I had a reputation as the go-to person for information and assistance on oral health issues.

These activities merely skim the surface of my life as a state representative; it was a life I relished. When my late husband Bob encouraged me to run for a state seat, he said I'd like the job because it was about helping people. And indeed, I loved every minute of the job—I loved being able to help people who didn't know where to turn in emergencies, loved being a voice for those who couldn't speak for themselves, and loved being able to make a positive difference in the lives of so many. I loved the excitement of being in the State House with 199 other gregarious, high-energy legislators and their dedicated legislative aides, interns, and State House staff—all of whom worked long hours serving the people of Massachusetts. I enjoyed meeting advocates, lobbyists, and the people who came to tell us about their issues. It was a privilege to work with so many high-caliber people.

When I was first elected, colleagues advised me to focus on a few issues in order to prevent "burnout." Yes, I was worn down by the extensive requests and issues I wanted to address. But how could I ignore requests for help in passing legislation that would make air, water, and soil cleaner for our children and grandchildren? How could I not get involved with policies to help the ill, the elderly, and the disabled? How could I turn away requests from hard-working good people who needed information, assistance in cutting through bureaucratic red tape, or who just needed to vent to someone who cared? I reached a point when I could no longer keep up with all these important requests even though my aide and I worked hard at it daily. An additional aide would have really helped. The speakers had given additional aides in return for loyalty. I guess I wasn't among the loyal ranks.

The legislature had great potential to improve life for all people in Massachusetts: funding more mental health care to prevent addictions and suicides; creating regulations for lowering toxins in our air to reduce asthma problems and reducing toxins in food and other products to prevent cancer; increasing staffing of agencies like the Department of Revenue to ensure less fraud. These and other preventative measures could have saved money, heartbreak, and lives. I would still be working to serve the people of Massachusetts if power and money were not driving the legislative agendas.

Chapter 7: People Deserve to be Heard at Committee Hearings

In every legislative session, the business of the State House begins with a January deadline for the Senate and House clerks' offices to receive around 5,000 bills. To get a better sense of this, let me explain how the committee process works and how it is controlled.

Examining the committee process

Some of the bills that come in are new files, like the very first bill I filed to make gamma beta hydroxide (better known as Ecstasy) a controlled illegal substance. Some, like my bill to license naturopathic physicians, are refiled many times. There are also late-file bills. (The joint rules of the legislature specify both how bills are scheduled and what the committee deadlines are for voting on bills.)

I learned that, like other legislative rules, these rules can be suspended by a formal or informal vote. The clerks' offices, with oversight from the speaker and the senate president, sort these bills and assign them to appropriate committees for consideration, such as the joint committees on education; financial services; environment, transportation; public safety and homeland security; public health; state administration; labor and workforce development; insurance; and many more. Next, each bill is assigned a committee hearing, when it is evaluated for its merits and given a yea, nay, or study vote by the respective committee members. Committee hearings are a vehicle for determining a bill's merits. Both representatives and senators sit on the various joint committees and listen as the people of Massachusetts, lobbyists, advocates, and guest experts speak for or against each bill.

Every two years on the first Wednesday of January following the November election, legislators take the oath of office before they are officially able to perform their duties. The first matter of business, after being sworn in, is to vote for their respective leaders for the two-year session.

House members vote for speaker of the house, and senators vote for senate president. Often, months earlier, candidates for house speaker and senate president will lobby prospective elected members for their votes. They fight fiercely for supporters even before elections determine who will win representative seats in the 160 house districts and senate seats in the forty senatorial districts. Deals are made between those competing for the position and those who can deliver the necessary votes.

In April 1996, prior to my first election, Speaker Charlie Flaherty resigned as speaker. (He had been convicted of a felony and left before the end of his term.) On April 9, 1996, Democrat Thomas Finneran beat Democrat Richard Voke in a speaker's race by making a deal with the Republicans, who gave Finneran the edge he needed to defeat Voke. In return for their support, the Republicans, although in the minority, received a lot of power and had a lot of influence under Finneran's rule. Nine years later, as Speaker Finneran prepared to leave the State House, it was rumored that he had brokered an agreement that helped his successor Sal DiMasi (D-Boston), win the coveted leadership position in what was shaping up to be a close speaker's race between Democrats Sal DiMasi from Boston and John Rogers from Norwood. Just days before the vote was taken, John Rogers withdrew and DiMasi won unanimously, except for a single dissenting vote by Representative Cory Atkins from Acton. The reason for DiMasi's overwhelming election was that he and Rogers had made an agreement wherein DiMasi would help Rogers succeed him as the next speaker. The deal between DiMasi and Rogers negated the opportunity for many individual reps to participate in the behind-the-scenes deal-making that was and is often part of the process of selecting a speaker. Because Rogers withdrew from the race, DiMasi didn't need the support of a group of us who had organized ourselves into a block of votes in an attempt to gain some influence in electing our new speaker. This, we had hoped, would have given us more support from the new speaker.

In the 2009 speaker's race, after I had left the legislature, it seemed that DiMasi didn't give Rogers the help he had agreed to after all because Robert DeLeo (D-Winthrop), beat John Rogers as Sal DiMasi's successor. Since I was no longer in the legislature I don't know what happened to their agreement.

The speaker of the house is a much coveted position because the person in the job wields great power in the state. The first thing a speaker does when he (Massachusetts has never had a female speaker) assumes leadership is to present the rule changes that will mark his style of leadership. The Manual of the General Court (updated each two-year term) dictates how the members of the Mass-achusetts Legislature carry out the law-making and budget-building during the two-year legislative session. The rule book is thick, and the rules—written by lawyers—are complicated. Although rule changes are subject to a roll call vote, they are generally supported by all who voted for the speaker. As I mentioned previously, a vote against the rules is viewed as a lack of confidence in the speaker, and as a result, you begin the year on the wrong side of the speaker.

Representatives want to be viewed favorably by the speaker because the speaker has tight control over the House of Representatives. He decides upcoming committee assignments and pretty much what gets into the budget, what bills come before the House for a vote, and which bills pass. The speaker also determines the number of aides each rep has to assist with committee work, the annual budget process, district needs, and constituent services. Likewise, the speaker determines parking spaces and office locations. The choicest offices overlook Boston Common, and the least desirable spaces have no windows and very little work area.

As a woman, I always had a parking space in the garage under the State House. Most male legislators parked in the garage under the McCormick Building across the street from the State House. I appreciated this benefit during inclement weather because it was so easy to walk through the building to my car before the almost two-hour commute home.

Usually, over the next few weeks of a session, the speaker

asks all members what three committees they would most like to serve on. He then proceeds to assign the members to the committees and selects their chairs and vice chairs. Speakers often make these selections based on how important an individual rep was to his, the speaker's, election and on the speaker's assessment of each rep's past and potential loyalty in voting the way the speaker wants. The present base salary for a Massachusetts State Rep is $62,500 a year, with an increase every other year based on the median salary increase in Massachusetts. However, those selected to be part of leadership receive an additional $7,500 or $15,000 a year, depending on the importance of the position. Some of these positions are: speaker pro tem, majority leader, majority whip, minority leader, minority whip, committee chair, and division leaders. Maintaining a leadership position also requires loyalty to the speaker.

At the beginning of each session of my five two-year terms, I requested an appointment to the committee on health care or the committee on public health. I believed (and still believe) that life is precious and fragile and that good health is a priority over financial, educational, and career success. Each term, I was appointed to serve on the joint committee on health care, which later, in Speaker Finneran's 2002 rules, was divided into three health care committees: the committee on public health, the committee on health care finance, and the committee on mental health.

This change gave more attention to the different aspects of health care while we were working on the important 2006 Massachusetts Health Care Reform Bill. However, it added more red tape that made it more difficult to follow the details of this bill as it was drafted. It also created more hurdles in the process of passing other health-related bills, and it created two more paid chair positions for the speaker to give out. I am proud of our Massachusetts Health Care Reform Bill that became the model for President Obama's Affordable Care Act, but I believe both laws were a beginning that required work addressing the cost and quality associated with these major health care delivery reforms.

Another committee I served on was the committee on state administration, which considered bills on public construction, state investments and properties, state symbols, state procurements, and state contracts. While initially unfamiliar with most issues before the Joint State Administration Committee, I found it to be a very interesting and important committee when it came to issues about investments for state pensions in tobacco and other companies and labor issues between unions, contractors, and subcontractors for public projects. I was also appointed to the committee on elder affairs, which dealt with nursing homes, home care, elder abuse, end-of-life issues, and other issues pertaining to senior citizens. Serving on these three committees was a big responsibility because the issues we considered had an impact on the lives of the six million people in Massachusetts. I tried to learn as much as I could about each issue that came before us.

The committee chair and her/his staff schedule bill hearings by related topics and create a calendar for the hearings. Some of the health care topics addressed while I served were HMO (Health Maintenance Organizations), managed care insurance, Lyme disease, stem cell research, environmental health, asthma and diabetes, tobacco use, nursing homes, preparedness for contagious disease control, prescription drug costs, oral health, and end-of-life. These hearings were typically held in Rooms A-1, A-2, B-1, or B-2; but when the subjects were complex or controversial (such as managed care insurance, Lyme disease, and end-of-life) and required more seating, they were held in the Gardner Auditorium, or outside the State House at one of the state colleges or other locations as determined by the chairperson.

As mentioned earlier, the hearings gave citizens an opportunity to express why they favored or opposed a bill. Everyone who "signs in" just before a hearing was (and is) given an opportunity to speak and provide written testimony. Written testimony is also accepted, usually a week or two, sometimes longer, after a hearing. During my ten years on the Health Care Committee, I don't recall missing more than ten of those countless committee hearings.

In fact, eager to attend my very first health care hearing in 1997, I expressed my regrets to Speaker Finneran when he invited me and three male colleagues (the four of us had been elected class officers by our legislative Class of '97) to join him for lunch at Locke-Ober's Restaurant. As a representative of my almost 40,000 constituents, I felt my first responsibility was to learn as much as I could about issues before voting on them. I had never heard of Locke-Ober's, a famous restaurant in downtown Boston frequented by judges, lawyers, senators, cardinals, and businessmen of high stature. Locke-Ober's, which didn't allow women in the downstairs dining room until 1970, was just down the hill from the State House and had been an historic and convenient place for power-brokers and deal-makers to meet. Later the restaurant across the street from the State House, the Golden Dome (now called the 21st Amendment) was the place to make a deal.

Instead of dining in comfort with the Speaker and colleagues, I ate my brown bag lunch and participated in my first health care committee hearing. And I would participate in hundreds more of these as well as hearings on many other issues during my ten years in the legislature. The following short list shows just a sample of the breadth and importance of only a few of the heartbreaking stories I listened to during those health care committee hearings.

- Travis Roy, the young Boston University hockey player, who became paralyzed after an injury during his first collegiate game, testified in favor of stem cell research.
- A forty-five-year-old husband and father with ALS (Lou Gehrig's disease) sat stiffly in his wheelchair, catching breaths through his ventilator, and told us about the need to collect data about pockets of ALS outbreaks in locations around Massachusetts.
- The president of the Massachusetts Nurses Association, who had contracted HIV/AIDS when she was accidentally stuck by a contaminated needle, spoke on behalf of a bill to require safe handling of used medical sharps.

- Parents from my district and other districts throughout Massachusetts pled for help for their young adult children addicted to OxyContin and their resulting heroin addictions—and told us of how insurance companies failed to provide appropriate coverage for rehabilitation.
- Families testified about the devastating damage that undiagnosed or misdiagnosed Lyme disease had caused their loved ones and of the need for policy and protocols regarding the testing for and successful treatment of Lyme using high levels of antibiotics.
- Public health officials testified about the dangers of a SARS (Severe Acute Respiratory Syndrome caused by a coronavirus) epidemic and of how unprepared our medical facilities would be to meet the needs of the afflicted during an epidemic.
- Midwives spoke about the benefits of breast milk for babies' short- and long-term health as they sought legislation banning the marketing of baby formula products via free product samples to new mothers leaving hospital maternity wards with their babies.
- Senior citizens told us about driving to Canada in order to afford prescription drugs that were researched and developed through grants funded by U.S. tax dollars.
- Psychiatrists explained the harm of substituting generic drugs for the specific complex compounded drugs required by their patients to control complicated mental illnesses.
- Oncologists expressed their concerns for teenagers and children who were being targeted by tobacco companies in their marketing of new flavored cigarettes.
- Nurses returned year after year asking for safe staffing legislation to fight mandatory overtime and unsafe patient-nurse ratios that taxed their ability to remain alert and make well-considered decisions regarding their patients' care.

I sat for hours in these hearings, sometimes with only the chair and one other committee member. As many committee sessions dragged on, we were sometimes the only ones who remained to listen as people told of their ongoing struggles living with health care issues. (Maybe my listening and putting myself in their shoes are the reasons why I never take good health for granted.) Other legislators' reasons for poor attendance at these hearings included conflicts with other committee hearings, or legislative appointments or workloads. But sometimes the hearings just weren't a priority for these chronically absent legislative members.

People who took time off from work, fought the highways and Boston traffic, paid to park, and sat for hours waiting for an opportunity to express their concerns deserved to have someone hear of their experiences, their expertise, and to attend to their requests, and I would do that, even if my own back and bottom hurt from the hours of sitting in hearings. The taxpayers who paid our salaries and our pensions deserved to have us listen to all sides of issues so we could vote in their best interests. During my ten years, I felt it was the least I could do to listen to the people's needs. (By the way, I did finally get to eat at Locke-Ober's one night in January 2000, when my friend George Lynch took me there for dinner.) I often wonder why life has been so good for me and so tragic for others.

Some bills seem to be "no-brainers" to the public, but people with first-hand involvement or more in-depth information may have strong reservations against passage of a bill and will request to meet with the chair. One such bill was the Baby Safe Haven Bill, a very popular measure that was touted as a way to save unwanted newborn babies from being abandoned in restrooms or dumpsters.

Rep. Tom O'Brien (D-Halifax), who sponsored this bill, and I, who had reservations about it, requested such a meeting with the chair of the Children's Caucus, Rep. Stephen LeDuc (D-Marlboro). At the meeting were Tom's constituents, Mr. and Mrs. Morrissey from Kingston, who argued passionately for the bill, my own constituent

Kim Stevens from Massachusetts Families for Kids, and Dr. Ellen White, an emergency room doctor at Children's Hospital. My constituent and Dr. White had serious reservations concerning the Baby Safe Haven Bill.

At the meeting, Kim and Dr. White explained why they opposed the bill. Both had many years of professional experience with abandoned and abused babies; they felt that passage of the Babies Safe Haven Bill would give the impression that a very complex problem could be remedied with safe places to bring babies born from unwanted pregnancies. They argued that mothers who abandon babies are often so troubled that they are in a state of denial about their pregnancies. Others are under the influence of drugs or they're afraid for their lives because they live in abusive situations. A frightened, young, unwed mother might think it would be easier to deliver the baby on her own and then drop the baby anonymously at a fire or police station than to tell her parents. This bill, they said, could encourage choices that could be life-threatening to the mother and the baby and have long-term consequences for the child. The bill also was a "feel good" piece of legislation that put a Band-Aid on the issue of child protection and mental health that needed to be addressed from many angles. The public would think we had solved the problem, when in reality we might be making it far more complicated.

The compromise we reached before the bill, called the Safe Haven Act of Massachusetts, was passed in 2004 was the inclusion of sunset language (language in a bill that provides for an automatic repeal of the entire or sections of a law once a specific date is reached) that called for an evaluation of the success of the program after the first two years, along with provisions for outreach to pregnant women about prenatal support available to them. Taking the unpopular stand to delay passage of this bill would result, I believed, in a bill more beneficial to mothers and babies. However, my position on this bill also gave my political opponents sound bites to use against my re-election. At an annual Whitman Town Meeting, a Republican woman

*At a New England Patriots event (L-R): Kathy & Bob Teahan
with Ann & Bob O'Connell*

*"Trooper" helps Ed Teahan
hold sign*

RE-ELECT
R E P R E S E N T A T I V E
Kathleen M.
Teahan

"For six years I have dedicated my full-time attention and energy to representing you in the Massachusetts Legislature. It has been an honor and a privilege to work with you to improve life for people in our community."

RELENTLESSLY LOCAL

- Increased the amount of state funding for education coming to the 7th Plymouth District by 40%.
- Implemented 31 tax cuts for families and businesses.
- Brought state funding for water, sewer and road projects to the district.
- Helped seniors pay for prescription drugs with the Advantage Pharmacy Program.
- Secured public safety funds to maintain well-trained and well-equipped police, fire and emergency personnel.

"Kathy Teahan works tirelessly on the issues we care about: education, the economy and our health care system."
Robert F. McCarthy, Plymouth County Register of Probate
and former State Senator from East Bridgewater

Campaign Card

Campaign volunteers holding signs in Whitman Center

Campaign button

Kathy with Legislative Aide Edna Donoghue (left)

*Kathy with Legislative Aide
Mike Power*

*Intern Meg Haines-Boyd
(left) and Legislative Aide
Jennifer Lynch-Horton*

*Kathy at the podium at
Plymouth County Farm Bureau
Meet Your Legislators Day*

Toll House Cookie Day celebration at Whitman Town Hall

Kathy with the late Tim Russert (NBC News Washington Bureau Chief and host of Meet the Press)

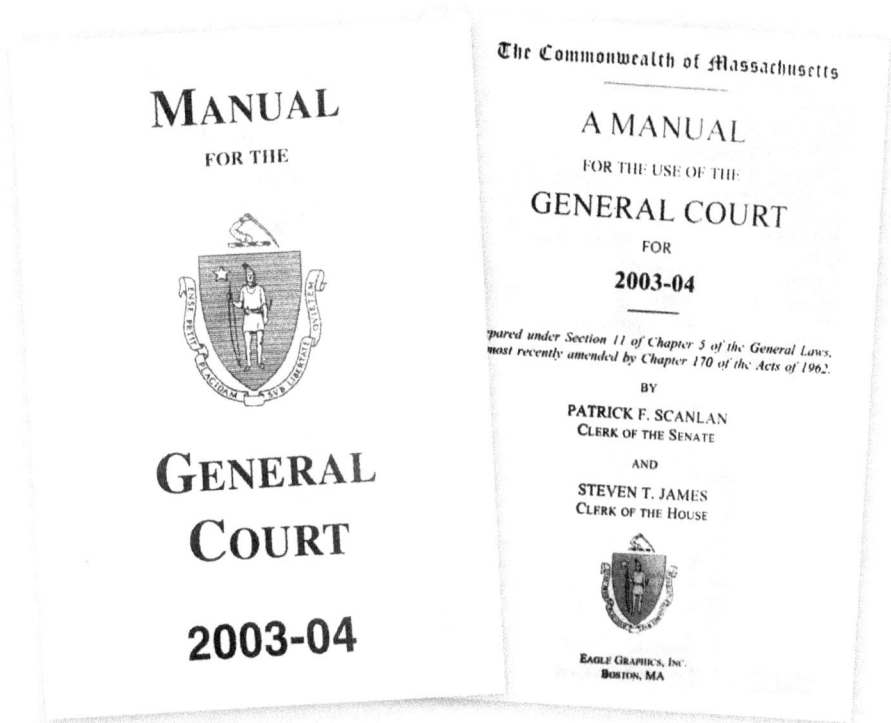

MANUAL

FOR THE

GENERAL COURT

2003-04

The Commonwealth of Massachusetts

A MANUAL

FOR THE USE OF THE

GENERAL COURT

FOR

2003-04

pared under Section 11 of Chapter 5 of the General Laws, most recently amended by Chapter 170 of the Acts of 1962.

BY

PATRICK F. SCANLAN
CLERK OF THE SENATE

AND

STEVEN T. JAMES
CLERK OF THE HOUSE

EAGLE GRAPHICS, INC.
BOSTON, MA

The legislative "rules" book

Veterans Oral History Project interview with veterans Stan Litchfield from Whitman VFW Post 697, WWII Veteran Harry Blakeman, Kathy, and WWII Veteran Clint Jenkins

~ 81 ~

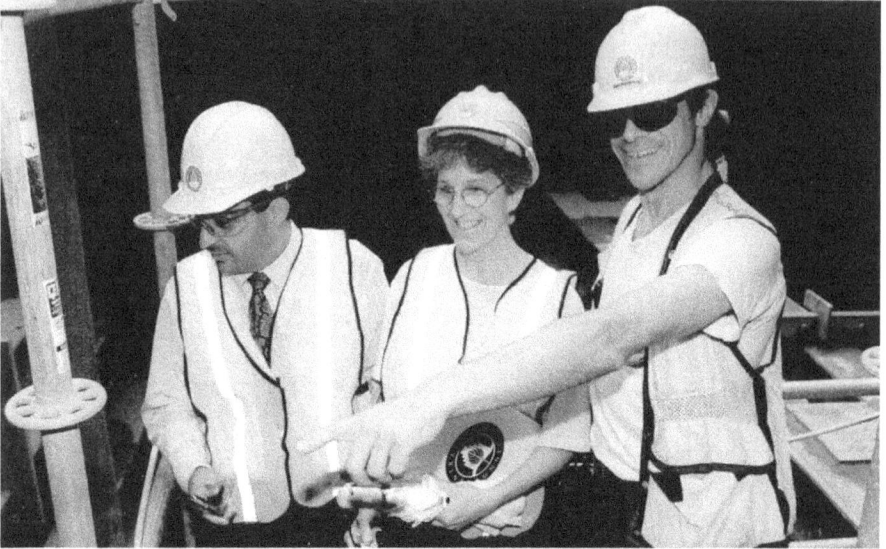

Kathy learns about "slurry" from contractors on the
Central Artery Project tunnel construction

At a hearing on Oral Health issues in Brockton (L-R): Mary Foley,
MA Director of Oral Health; intern; Christine Canavan,
Brockton State Representative; Kathy; and Helene Bednash,
MA Dept. of Public Health

Presentation of Special Commission on Oral Health Report

Mary Foley, RDH, Director of Oral Health at MA Dept. of Public Health; Burton Edelstein, DDS; Kathy; Allison Staton, Advocate, Health Care for All

Kathy; Myron Allukian, DDS; James B. Bramson, DDS

Crowded hearing room for release of report:
The Oral Health Crisis in Massachusetts

Kathy and Senator Michael Morrisey (right) learn about train safety
from MBTA administrators for the opening of the Kingston/Boston
commuter rail line

Dedicated Abington supporters Jennifer Oriola, Kathy, Janet Oriola

Ava - In my world it would always be spring and things age would always be growing like me and everyone 4. would be nice to each other, friends and help each other and there would be no fighting. And if it snowed it would be pink and warm

Ava's drawing and thoughts for "If I were in Charge of the World"

brought up my opposition to the bill. During the Town Meeting (which was clearly not the place to explain all the hours of meetings and work I had done on this issue in the best interests of my constituents), she used my vote in an attempt to influence voters against me in an upcoming campaign.

A deeper dive into committees and bills

After a committee hearing, research staff for that committee would go to work analyzing the bills that were leadership priorities and, to some extent, House members' priorities. We would receive information from lobbyists, non-profit organizations, other states, lawyers, municipal and county workers, businesses, unions, and other interested parties. Sponsors and opponents of the bills would anxiously await the committee's executive session on their bill. After consideration by the chair and committee staff and, I believe, often with the speaker's supervision, the bill was "exec'd" (committee jargon for "moved") out of committee during the executive session. This consisted of the chair's reading the bill title and number, telling what the committee had decided to do with the bill, and then saying, "All in favor," and "All opposed."

We, as committee members, didn't actually vote on the bills. We had in front of us what the committee chair had decided to do with the bill. A member could express serious concerns to a chair or staff member prior to the actual vote, and chairs were very accommodating in listening to members. And, as with the Safe Haven Bill, they allowed us to bring people from our districts to their offices to discuss a bill. A rep could also try to stop a vote at the executive session, although this was frowned upon. Sometimes the bill was sent to a "study."

Actual studies look more closely at an issue, but in this case, more often, a study was a "nice" way to kill a bill. A bill could also receive an unfavorable vote from the committee's executive session— meaning the bill was dead until it was re-filed in a future session. If a bill got a favorable vote from the committee, the bill's sponsor had to track the bill usually through a long and tedious process, which included letters, phone calls, and requests for appointments to speak to chairs of different committees, such as the committee on rules; the committee on steering; policy and scheduling; the committee on bills in the third reading (where House Counsel analyzes the bill before its final reading for its potential duplication, constitutionality, wording and grammar, to fit appropriately into the Massachusetts General Laws); and the Ways and Means Committee—all before the bill could go to the House floor for a vote. My patience and perseverance came in handy during this process, which at times seemed like an obstacle course. Relationships with colleagues in leadership positions were and are very important because they open and close pathways to moving a bill closer to becoming law. While I got along well with my colleagues and worked very hard, I never made it into the inner leadership circle.

The House Ways and Means Committee is extremely important and powerful in Massachusetts because one of its tasks is to draft the annual House Budget, which determines how we distribute our tax dollars, tolls, and fees to meet the needs of our six million Massachusetts residents. Without funding, the best policies cannot come to fruition. For people in Massachusetts to live together in health and harmony, we need breathable air, clean drinking water, sewerage and rubbish disposal, healthy food supplies, safe roads, safe transit systems, high quality public safety, and good public schools. We need well-prepared and well-supported public health systems, as well as the energy and infrastructure to maintain and operate our electronics and airwaves.

After the governor's budget proposal is made public in January (and you can find it yourself on the mass.gov website), many lobbyists, advocates, and individuals visit representatives' offices, the House Ways and Means Committee, and the Speaker of the House, requesting help adding or restoring money for specific line items. My aides and I spent many hours listening to requests and reading letters and emails with requests. We organized a file-folder with requests that I would support by co-sponsoring amendments, and then in another folder, the amendments I filed along with arguments supporting these items. Without the wonderful organization of my aides, I would have had to dig my way out of piles of paperwork.

On the days of the formal House budget sessions, I had neat, well-organized three-ring notebooks with information about my amendments. Before each of our formal budget sessions began, the Ways and Means Committee would call a meeting in Room 348 of the members' lounge to inform the 160 representatives about which of the hundreds of filed amendments to the budget this committee had accepted and would bundle together accordingly for votes.

In this room there was an oval conference table with about a dozen chairs and a bench. About a hundred reps would stand three deep around the table, with several conversations going on at the same time—all of this making it very difficult to see and hear the information about our own amendments. This kind of disorganization was shocking to me and so different from the way I had organized my own teaching and legislative work. I was pretty disgusted with it because so much of the decision-making was done by just a few members and behind closed doors! If a rep didn't agree to the Ways and Means decision, she could pull her amendment and request a vote on it in the formal House budget session. However, this would "spot" the members. (See my earlier explanation of "spotting.") No colleague wanted to be in this tough position.

Chapter 8: Representing 40,000 Constituents

To create state representative districts, the population of Massachusetts (approximately 7.1 million) is divided by 160, the total number of state representatives. Each district has about 40,000 people who make up a constituency or body of citizens who elect and are served by a legislator. My district, the 7th Plymouth District, included Abington, East Bridgewater, and Whitman, with a little under 40,000 people. State senators in Massachusetts have roughly 160,000 constituents. Three senators, one from Brockton, one from Quincy, and one from Milton covered my district.

Constituent service is an important factor in winning re-election. It creates a direct connection between a legislator and the people in her/his district, and one of the key services a state rep can provide is cutting through the red tape of government bureaucracy. But before I could help my constituents with a state agency, I had to work hard at getting the whole alphabet soup of agencies straight in my mind. Here is a sample of that soup:

RMV (Registry of Motor Vehicles)
DMA (Division of Medical Assistance)
DPH (Department of Public Health)
EOHHS (Executive Office of Health and Human Service)
MEMA (Massachusetts Emergency Management Agency)
HUD (Department of Housing and Urban Development)
DUA (Department of Unemployment Assistance)
DEP (Department of Environmental Protection)
DOC (Department of Corrections)
DIV (Division of Insurance)
DCR (Department of Conservation and Recreation)
DOE (Department of Education)
EOE (Executive Office of Education)
DOT (Department of Transportation)

DOR (Department of Revenue)

DOI (Division of Insurance)

EOPSS (Executive Office of Public Safety and Security).

Each agency had an employee designated as legislative liaison. That person's job was to be a resource to legislators who received requests from constituents for assistance with an issue associated with that agency. Here are some samples of constituent pleas for help upon which I acted:

- Please support the Bill to Establish a Voter Confidentiality Address that would ensure privacy protection for abuse victims while enabling them to vote.

- Why had a teacher not received his Massachusetts Teacher Certificate one year after completing the required courses, passing the MTEL (Massachusetts Tests for Educator Licensure) exams, and submitting a comprehensive application?

- Is there help for a family whose home has been over-run with toxic mold, causing various illnesses in family members and the death of their young child?

- Why has a thirty-year-old woman born with fetal alcohol syndrome and other developmental disabilities received a letter stating she is no longer eligible for SSDI (Social Security Disability Insurance) and that she owes the government $7,000?

- Why can't a good family raising four healthy, happy children of their own, adopt two half-sisters who have been living with an elderly grandmother no longer capable of caring for them?

- Why do parents with children addicted to OxyContin and heroin receive more information and help from peer groups of other parents than from state or federal programs?

- Why aren't there more schools of nursing to address our shortage of nurses and wait-lists of applicants with high academic averages?

- Why does the Massachusetts Parole Board continue to postpone a parole hearing for an inmate with exemplary behavior?
- Why hasn't the Massachusetts Division of Insurance scheduled an appeal hearing more than a year after a decision about an auto accident claim?

When I left the legislature, I filled three eighty-gallon paper-recycling receptacles with thousands of pages of constituent request forms to be discarded because they contained the personal information of the people we helped. Each form represented a part of someone's life story that she/he had entrusted to me. Along with the honor of being elected as a state representative came my sacred commitment to listen to and do my best to help my constituents. One story that I will never forget concerned a ten-year-old boy, David Stuart, and his father.

David Stuart and the Catastrophic Illness in Children Relief Fund

During my very first term in the legislature, Helen Zak, a friend from Whitman, called to ask for my help—not for herself but for a ten-year-old boy with cancer, the nephew of her friend. This boy, David Stuart, had lived in Rockland, a neighboring town, but had recently moved with his father and two sisters to Sandwich. Whenever someone outside a representative's district requests help, it is a courtesy to work with the person's own district rep, so I contacted Representative Ruth Provost from Sandwich and Bob Nyman from Rockland. Together, we worked on the Stuart case. I stayed involved because as a mother, I felt the heartache of a parent in this situation.

David's father had been self-employed as a carpenter. He and his wife were divorced, and he had custody of their three children. When David was diagnosed with cancer and required many appointments for treatments and tests, his father took time off from work when other family members could not accompany David. Being self-employed, Mr. Stuart was no longer making enough money to pay for a family health insurance plan, so his children became eligible for MassHealth, and he went without insurance for himself. After David's two years of treatments, his doctors at Children's Hospital, Boston, said that there was nothing more they could do for him but that a new treatment for David's condition was available at a hospital in California.

David's MassHealth insurance refused to cover the hospital costs for this treatment because the treatment was experimental. David's father, fighting to keep his son alive, appealed the MassHealth decision. Because he was very nervous speaking in front of people and because he could not afford a lawyer to present David's case, David's father asked if I would accompany him to the hearing and help him fight for his son's case. I wasn't a lawyer, but I was a mother and a fighter, so I agreed. Walking down the Park Street hill from the State House, through the crowds of shoppers, students, tourists, business professionals, lawyers, and the homeless filling the downtown streets, I found the MassHealth offices in a new building on the corner of Washington and Boylston Streets. The weather forecast had been for strong winds and heavy rain later in the afternoon, and the wind was already increasing as I entered the building.

Mr. Stuart and his two sisters were waiting for me in the lobby, and together we took the stairs up to the second floor hearing room, which was a windowless box with blank cream-colored walls. Our green metal chairs hugged the walls and were placed on the outside of two rectangular tables arranged in an L shape. At the front of the room, a stenographer sat at a small desk with her steno machine and a telephone. Near her was the MassHealth official. I sat at the table with my papers and notes, and the Stuart family sat around the table's corner and against the wall. Representative Ruth Provost (D-Sandwich), who arrived shortly after the meeting began, sat directly across from me and mouthed several good ideas to me during the hearing.

No smiles or attempts to make us feel comfortable were offered by the MassHealth officials. Representative Bob Nyman

(Rockland) arrived late due to other commitments. The hearing lasted more than two hours, and I used every argument I could think of. Specialists from Boston's Children's Hospital recommended David for the treatments available in California, knowing there were no 100-percent certain cures for cancer in general, and all treatments would be experimental. Some children with cancer similar to David's had responded well to the treatment in California. Our state, Massachusetts, one of the richest states in one of the wealthiest countries in the world, with billions of dollars spent each year on health care, could certainly find money to help this one sick child.

Ruth, Bob, and I left the hearing without a decision and with heavy hearts, concerned for a family having to fight for treatments for their beautiful son, who should have been playing ball and running around the neighborhood with friends, as ten year-olds do. Bob telephoned his legislative aide who drove down to pick us up because of the hurricane-related torrents that had developed over Boston during the hearing. We jumped over large puddles of windswept rain to hop into the car that would take us back to the magnificent State House, a symbol of our government, a Commonwealth where each person supposedly had the right to the blessings of life, liberty, and the pursuit of happiness.

After a long and agonizing week, Mr. Stuart received a notice that his appeal for MassHealth coverage for David's California hospitalization had been denied. When Mr. Stuart called, it was hard for me to find the words to express my sadness. How could our state have turned its back on this child? Neither Ruth, Bob, nor I felt very proud to represent Massachusetts on that day. Ruth suggested we call Senator Terry Murray who was serving her fourth term in the Senate and was a strong advocate for children and others in need. Terry said there was nothing she could do to change the appeal denial, but as I sat in her office the next day, I listened while she enlisted help from Marjorie Claprood, a former state rep. Senator Murray also called contacts she knew at the World Cup Golf Tournament that was taking place then in Brookline, Massachusetts. After approximately two hours on the telephone, Terry and Marjorie had raised the funds for David's hospitalization and had received a donation from Senator Ted Kennedy to cover travel expenses for David and his dad.

Children's Hospital communicated with the California hospital and all the arrangements were made. Mr. Stuart and David went to California. Initial treatments were delayed a few weeks because David's blood counts were off. During the three months or so of treatments, Mr. Stuart would call every once in a while to give us an update on David's progress. It was pretty much a rollercoaster ride of ups and downs with infections and low white-cell blood counts.

Meanwhile back in Massachusetts, David's story had received a lot of local media coverage, and people were questioning the lack of funding for David's needs. Marcia Huttner, a licensed social worker, saw one of the newspaper stories and called to tell me about a program in New Jersey that provided financial assistance for families whose children were experiencing illnesses or conditions not covered by private or public insurance or other sources. Senator Murray, and Reps. Provost, Nyman, and I filed legislation to create a similar fund in Massachusetts, financed through an annual surcharge of $1 per employee, paid by employers subject to the Unemployment Compensation Law. This bill passed and created the Catastrophic Illness in Children Relief Fund. When David completed his treatments, he and his father returned to Sandwich, both weakened from the battle. Sadly, David's cancer worsened, and he died soon after at twelve years old.

The Stuart family's tragedy, however, had been the catalyst for the creation of a new program offering hope for other children. Several years after David's death, I attended a celebration of the 5th Anniversary of the Catastrophic Illness in Children Relief Fund. It was attended by many families of severely disabled children who had been helped by the fund inspired by David's needs.

One mother read from her letter about the fund: "After a long battle of approximately one and a half years, our son finally has the wheelchair his doctor prescribed for him. The Massachusetts Division of Medical Assistance denied an expensive wheelchair with a standing option that Jacob's muscular dystrophy doctor was adamantly seeking for Jacob. [These electric wheelchairs move a person's body to a secure upright position that is beneficial to circulation, muscle integrity, prevention of sores, and an improvement in self-esteem. They cost from $5,000 to $50,000.] Thanks to the $4,890.53 paid by the Catastrophic Illness in Children Relief Fund, we picked up Jacob's chair on Halloween, and what a difference it has made in his life! The first week he wanted to watch me make supper. (He could never see what I was doing before when he was always in a seated position.) We made cookies together, but the best activity by far is being able to hug him while he was in a standing position. Wow!!! He was even able to help decorate the Christmas tree this year. Thank you so much and please keep us in your prayers." This fund continues to help children to this day.

The downside of redistricting

Another issue that affected our constituents was, and continues to be, redistricting, which can lead to gerrymandering (creating districts that benefit or hurt a political party or an individual official's election chances). Every ten years after the federal census is completed, the House and Senate examine the districts and realign them to adjust for population shifts. While I served, Massachusetts Speaker of the House Thomas Finneran created a new committee, the committee on election laws, to hear bills that would pertain to election issues such as redistricting legislation that would address district proportions. Other issues would involve voter registration, absentee ballots, and voter IDs—many of the same issues of major concern today.

Representative Carol Cleven, a popular Republican incumbent whose district covered all of Chelmsford, found that her district was to be divided into four segments, three of which were included in the abutting districts of three Democratic male incumbents. Carol had served the people of Chelmsford for sixteen years and was well-regarded in her district and in the House as a hardworking, honest, and dedicated public servant and an all-around good person. In a similar manner, two other districts represented by two liberal Democratic women were also modified substantially, making their re-election more difficult and giving the female representatives new groups of constituents to serve. I was upset and disillusioned that redistricting was apparently being used to try to remove three women from our already low numbers of women in the House. Representative Cleven decided not to run for reelection in her gerrymandered district. This redistricting plan was also found to have hurt minority populations. It led to a court case in which the speaker was found guilty of perjury. This practice of gerrymandering protects political incumbents against challengers and provides white candidates an advantage over candidates of color. To stop this, Massachusetts must pass a law creating an independent group to redraw the map of political districts where needed after the federal census every ten years.

Attention to constituents arises again here as a very important factor in the re-election of incumbent legislators. Because there are two sides to every issue, each time a legislator votes she makes some people happy and upsets others. Aiding constituents in my district in various ways helped grow my popularity even with voters who did not agree with my particular stand on an issue. But more importantly, at the end of each day, my reward was knowing that I had helped lighten someone's struggles.

Chapter 9: "There But for the Grace of God..."

Walking has always been a habit of mine, probably going back to when my family didn't own a car during my first seventeen years growing up in Whitman.

While in the legislature, I would often take a brief walk outside the State House to clear my head. Early mornings, before my drive to Beacon Hill, I would walk down Harvard Street to the library with our golden retriever, Archie. Trying to set a good example for beautifying our town and with inspiration from a dedicated environmentalist, Michael Celona, I picked up litter along the way. During those walks, I sometimes saw a faded maroon van parked beside the chain-link fence that bordered the parking lot behind the Holy Ghost Catholic Church. Other times it was parked under a tall pine tree in the center of St. James Cemetery, or in the parking lots of the American Legion Hall or The Office, a small barroom in the center of town. Patty Hill (not her real name), who in the 1960s, had walked the same high school hallways with me, now lived with her German Shepherd in that faded maroon van.

Early in my first term, Larry Roache, an active member of the Whitman Democratic Town Committee, who along with his wife Kathy had helped me a lot in both my losing and successful campaigns, asked if I would try to help Patty. Patty had graduated from Whitman-Hanson Regional High School with Larry a couple of years before I did, and her sister was in my sister Eileen's class. Patty's family had moved to Whitman from Boston in the early 1960s along with many city families who did not like the court-ordered school busing intended to integrate Boston schools. The Hills lived in the Homeland Park development, which consisted of about a hundred nice-looking new homes built on cement slabs, on the wetlands just off Route 14 in Whitman. Patty was an average student, a polite kid, and she got along well enough with her classmates.

I met with Patty and learned she was disabled as a result of several bouts of cancer and alcoholism. While she might have qualified for housing assistance, there were few, if any, places that would have allowed her to keep her dog. (Sometimes when the rest of the world seems to turn its back on you, a dog is more than your best friend; he's your salvation. How indeed do you walk away from the creature that loves you unconditionally and gives you a reason to live?)

I talked to housing advocates, directors of various housing authorities, social workers, and staff of the Massachusetts Department of Housing and Community Development. In the late 1990s, there was little if any available public housing assistance in Massachusetts, and none for a woman with a large dog. All I could do was join Fr. Curran, an elderly priest from Holy Ghost Parish, Larry Roache and Patty's other friends and give Patty five or ten dollars at the end of the month when she needed it for gas, food, or maybe booze. As we so clearly saw during the Covid-19 Pandemic, there is still a great need for assistance for the Patties of the Commonwealth.

In 1999 it was determined that two homeless people who lived in the abandoned Worcester Cold Storage Warehouse accidentally started the fire that killed six Worcester firefighters. The firefighters gave their lives while searching the old warehouse for homeless people reported to be living in that abandoned six-story building. The two homeless people living there were later found to have mental disabilities and were not in the warehouse at the time of the fire. One of them, Julie Ann Barnes, had a twin sister who had been adopted into a wonderful family in Maine. Julie, who remained in foster care, was abandoned by "the system" at age eighteen when she aged out of foster care. (Because I was a member of a special commission on adoption, I knew that Julie was one of approximately 600 teens who aged out of foster care in Massachusetts every year.) The stark fact was that Julie's shelter in the abandoned cold storage warehouse had contributed to the death of six firefighters and the sorrow we all suffered from this tragedy.

I still think often of the lives, heartache, and money that might have been spared if we had done a better job for our homeless neighbors in Massachusetts and throughout the world.

My years of advocacy for constituents with housing needs brought me into contact with experts like Nancy Curtin from South Shore Housing Assistance, who had been working on solutions to our housing problems for decades. Year after year, I saw these experts unsuccessfully lobby for additional funding of successful programs like the Rental Assistance for Families in Transition (RAFT) program that helps people who can prove financial eligibility get an apartment, rent a home, or stay in their own homes by paying a late rent or utility bill or paying a security deposit and a first month's rent. RAFT was a way that working families could get that little boost needed to move into an affordable apartment or keep their home after an illness, accident, death, or unemployment reduced their income. Instead of waiting until families were homeless and sheltering them in motels or putting them on long lists for public housing, helping them stay in their apartments or homes made sense. Despite information that proved RAFT and similar programs would be cost-efficient for the Commonwealth, funding for increased homelessness prevention didn't happen until long after I had left the legislature.

In 2008, the year after I left the legislature, Governor Duval Patrick and the legislature budgeted funds to create more housing and more homelessness prevention programs. Governor Patrick showed an understanding of what I had learned from housing advocates about the need for supportive housing programs, such as job training, childcare and more assistance for the elderly, veterans, and our mentally and physically disabled.

Every Christmas and Hanukkah holiday season, people come together through their churches, synagogues, The Home for Little Wanderers, Toys for Tots, The Pine Street Inn, St. Francis House, Rosie's Place, the Greater Boston Food Pantry, and many other charitable organizations, to help the homeless in our communities.

We are a community of good people who want to help those sleeping on park benches, in city doorways and over grates, and in abandoned warehouses, cars, and vans.

I feel that government can and should, in a comprehensive, caring, and cost-efficient way, help house people who find themselves in complicated financial situations. As the saying goes, "There but for the grace of God, go I."

Chapter 10: Creating an Emerald Necklace through the Suburbs

Have you ever heard of the Bay Circuit Trail?

The Bay Circuit Trail concept originated in 1929 in order to add a second strand to the "Emerald Necklace" that Frederick Law Olmstead began creating in 1878 and completed in 1900. The goal of the original Emerald Necklace was to ensure that Boston area families had easy access to the health benefits of parks and natural open spaces.

The goal of the "Outer Emerald Necklace" was the same, except it was to benefit people in the communities that were growing outside of the immediate Boston area. During the worldwide COVID-19 pandemic, we realized more than ever just how important nature and public spaces for hiking and walking are to our physical and mental well-being. Whenever I start to feel down or out of energy, a short walk in the fresh air does wonders for my attitude. Today, the Bay Circuit Trail extends over 230 miles from Plum Island on the North Shore to Kingston Bay, Duxbury, on the South Shore. Many people have hiked its full length, through thirty-four towns and cities. But when I left the legislature in 2007, there remained a couple of segments of the old rail bed that were obstructed from public use. Unfortunately, one of those was in East Bridgewater, a town that was part of my district.

My involvement with this issue began one day in 1997 during my first term, when three outdoorsmen: Alan French, visionary and leader in developing the Bay Circuit Trail; Howard Wilbur, trail advocate and my constituent; and Phil Clemens, conservationist and trail advocate from Hanson—asked me to help them acquire surplus railroad property that would fill the East Bridgewater gap in the Bay Circuit Trail. As they explained what they were trying to accomplish, I thought: What a great idea and what an asset to the community! Being a member of the Joint Committee on Public Health had taught me how valuable a project like this could be to the long-term health of the citizens in our Commonwealth.

A scary statistic from "Losing Ground," a Massachusetts Audubon Society report, showed that from 1995 to 1999, forty acres of land in Southeastern Massachusetts were lost every day to developers. This area is today still being developed, but at a reduced rate of 13.5 acres per day instead of forty, according to the sixth edition of "Losing Ground (2017-2020)." The lesson? Wait too long, and land ownership becomes so fragmented that we lose forever the opportunity to provide people with contiguous open space. (Even our forebears in the Massachusetts government demonstrated the value of public open space when, in 1634, officials purchased the parcel of land that became the Boston Common.) Open space offers so many benefits: exercise, fresh air, good health, heightened respect for the natural environment, and meeting nice people along the way. While serving on the Committee on Public Health, I saw epidemiological statistics on obesity and asthma that showed the value of having safe places where families could exercise bathed in sunlight and clean air amid natural surroundings.

Rising costs of gasoline added another driving force for completing the Bay Circuit Trail, as future workers and students sought alternative transportation to jobs; to the Intra-modal Transportation Center in Brockton (site of the Old Colony Rail Station, buses, and taxis); to the nearby Bridgewater State University, Massasoit Community College; and even to K-12 public schools. The trail held the potential for becoming a significant part of our community's transportation infrastructure while increasing the value of adjoining properties. Experiences that other communities had had with bike trails showed that trails increased property values for residents while bringing tourists to the area.

So of course, I wanted to help Alan, Howard, and Phil with the Bay Circuit project. It was a no brainer, a win-win situation! Who would oppose using these old rail beds to benefit future generations? The proposed two-mile East Bridgewater trail segment through pristine woods and along a river became a project that I grew to care about wholeheartedly throughout my years as a state rep and beyond. I attended several meetings at the State House that had been organized by Senator Pamela Resor (D-Acton), Senator Susan Tucker (D-Andover), and Representative Anne Paulsen (D-Belmont). These legislators supported the trail and worked on other bills to reduce pollution and protect our environment, and they led our lobbying efforts on behalf of the trail. These three women influenced the passage of favorable bills that affected funding and policy changes and made the acquisition of rail rights-of-way more attractive to communities, especially those with tight budgets, like East Bridgewater. At the time when the three gentlemen requested my help, the MBTA was selling this rail property for about $200,000, and the Town of East Bridgewater, along with the Old Colony Planning Council, could not afford, even with grants, to make the purchase.

Legislation we passed during subsequent years changed those circumstances. Some of the accommodations the legislature enacted in 2002 allowed cash-strapped towns to lease (instead of buying) the abandoned rail bed for ninety-nine years for $1. We also passed legislation that allowed cities and towns to designate the rail trail as a public way so communities would be protected from personal injury lawsuits by the town's umbrella liability insurance plan. We also worked out compromises with the MBTA to deal with the environmental liability associated with rail-related contamination, such as the use of arsenic to preserve railroad ties.

Rail Trail fight continues

For a few years, I met with the East Bridgewater Friends of Trails in the kitchenette at the town hall. If this group of dedicated, community-oriented people seemed particularly wholesome, it might have been because one of them, Howard Wilbur, reminded me of "Andy" in the popular *Andy Griffith* TV show set in the fictional idealized small town of Mayberry. Other members included retired first-grade teacher and Howard Wilbur's sister, Marjorie Winsor, Reverend

Margaret Wohlers and her twin eighteen-year-old sons who had been active Boy Scouts, an Appalachian Mountain Club member, Diane Phillips, and a couple of additional nature enthusiasts.

Opposing our earnest collective effort was an abutter. In 2002, after the several helpful MBTA policy changes, this small band of dedicated citizens pressed the local board of selectmen to move ahead on the acquisition, but the three-member board denied the request, effectively disallowing the two-mile gap of the Bay Circuit Trail to be completed in East Bridgewater. The proponents were discouraged, but they didn't give up. And neither did I.

Bridgewater State University had conducted a poll that showed ninety-five percent of East Bridgewater respondents supported town land acquisition and considered the preservation of open space to be a town priority. These poll results encouraged the East Bridgewater Friends of the Trails to circumvent the board of selectmen by going to the townspeople. My legislative aide Mike Power and I assisted them in their effort to petition town meeting voters to make their wishes known to the selectmen.

One of the first things this group needed to do was fill out and file an extensive application so it could be considered a formal federal 501(c)(3) charity that could raise money to support information fliers and an audio-visual presentation. None of us had the expertise or experience to complete the application, but this was accomplished with generous help from a State House lawyer from the Joint Committee on Revenue staff. (Having access to such knowledgeable and supportive people proved both amazing and helpful.) Mike and I also drafted a town meeting article that requested the formation of a trail feasibility study group, and we developed strong arguments to support the article.

Although the town gave overwhelming support to our request for a study group, the conservation commission controlled the appointments to the study group. The group proved to be slow to meet and to act; at the 2003 Annual Town Meeting, the study group asked for and received approval to extend their study. (Delays are often the way to stop actions by discouraging volunteers.) Then, in 2005, an abutter filed a lawsuit against the MBTA, stating that this property, which had been taken by the government through eminent domain, should not be transferred to another party when it was no longer used for the initial intended public benefit, which he declared was for railroad use.

The rep gets a subpoena!

I had strongly supported the East Bridgewater segment of the Bay Circuit Trail, but I was still quite surprised when a local sheriff knocked on my door one day and handed me a deposition subpoena, with its intimidating words, "YOU ARE HEREBY COMMANDED." I spent the week after receiving the subpoena preparing mentally for my upcoming appearance and sworn testimony at a lawyer's office in Boston. The abutter lost the case but filed several appeals. (I've learned that sometimes we need a lot of patience to see a project through to completion, and sometimes we don't even get to see the completion of the project that future supporters will finally bring to fruition.)

It took years of court time before the court declared its final denial of the abutter's case. To this day, I don't know the total cost to the people of Massachusetts for lawyers' fees and MBTA court expenses during its attempts to bring the East Bridgewater abandoned rail trail back under its authority and make it available for the public good as part of the Bay Circuit Trail. (Today, I wonder how many of our U.S. tax dollars have been wasted on legal battles that are government-initiated or spent defending the government in our highly litigious society!)

The Friends of East Bridgewater Trails continues to work to bring to fruition its dream of adding East Bridgewater's segment and completing the 300-mile Bay Circuit Trail, as a permanent trail corridor linking parks and open space, accessible to all. Thank goodness for the foresight of Frederick Law Olmsted and the dedication and perseverance of a small group of people who became the Friends of East Bridgewater Trails. May all our children and future generations reap the benefits of this trail! I am looking forward to future walks there myself.

Chapter 11: Keeping an Eye on Land Swaps

Land ownership and use is complicated and often controversial, so much so that we have the Massachusetts Land Court in Boston and registries of deeds in all of our counties to settle disputes and keep records of transactions. We have thousands of laws and regulations relating to sewage, sludge, realtors, surveying, engineering, and endangered species. We all need to keep a close eye on land deals.

The earliest land swap in my district occurred 350 years ago in East Bridgewater, not far from where I taught middle school students for nine years before entering politics. That deal was made on March 23, 1649, a quarter-century after the Pilgrims and the Native American Wampanoag tribe had become neighbors. The Wampanoag leaders sold the Pilgrim leaders forty-nine square miles of land that currently make up parts of the city of Brockton and the three towns of East and West Bridgewater, Bridgewater, and a small section of Duxbury. The deal was made at Sachem Rock, located at the Sachem Farm property, 355 Plymouth Street, in East Bridgewater. In exchange for their land, the Native Americans received seven coats, nine hatchets, eight hoes, twenty knives, four moose skins, ten and a half yards of cotton and twenty pounds sterling. The signers on the Pilgrim side were Myles Standish, Samuel Nash, and Constant Southworth. The sole signer for the Native Americans was Massasoit, chief of the Wampanoag Federation, who signed using the name Ousemequan (probably a birth name, emphasizing the personal nature of his participation). This event is commemorated in the East Bridgewater town seal and on its town flag.

In September of 1998, the Town of East Bridgewater repurchased thirty-two acres of the original property surrounding Sachem Rock from the estate of Dr. Donald B. Bannerman for one million dollars. The Native Americans probably had something different in mind when they sold the property. Co-existence perhaps? East Bridgewater had ideas for these thirty-two acres. (See Appendix 9.)

When I was elected to the legislature, my family and I lived in an antique Cape-style house on Harvard Street in Whitman. Our house had been built only sixty-five years after the original land sale at Sachem Rock. Rev. Whitmarsh of East Bridgewater had built the house in 1715 for his son. Back then, Harvard Street was just a well-trodden path between East Bridgewater and Old Abington.

The complexity of land sales

Shortly after I entered the legislature, an abandoned home, another antique Cape on three acres of land at 120 Harvard Street and just four houses down from ours, sold by auction, and I didn't know anything about it! There were no signs posted about the sale, and like the rest of my neighbors, I was too busy working and caring for my family to look into what had happened to the property. I learned of the auction only because a Whitman resident, Joe Saccone, called me to protest that the publicized winning bid was lower than the one he had planned to submit. Joe went to the original posted auction attended by only two other people besides himself. He asked the auctioneer if there were any federal liens on the property that he would take on with the bid. The auctioneer didn't have that information, so Joe did not bid. No one did. The auctioneer said another auction would be scheduled, but Joe never learned when it would occur. The property sold at auction for $53,000, considerably lower than the $70,000 that Joe had planned to bid and less than the loan balance at the time of the property's foreclosure. The remaining mortgage was held by Conti Mortgage Corporation, which was established in the state of Delaware and located at 338 South Warminster Road, One Conti Park, Hatboro, Pennsylvania. The sale didn't seem fair to Joe or to others in Whitman, so he asked for my help.

I spent a lot of time trying to track down the actual bidders on that property in my neighborhood. I called REMAX real estate offices because they had previously listed the property for sale. I called several banks, and I checked phone books and online sources but didn't get anywhere; and the mortgage company never returned my calls. I did learn that the person who represented the bidder worked for Winn Property Management, LLC, now located at 484 Tremont Street, Boston.

So one day, I crossed Bowden Street and went to the corporations section of the Office of the Secretary of State in the McCormick Building, where I asked for documents related to the LLC that purchased the property. Usually, state employees greet a state representative with friendliness and are eager to help. But in this office, I met workers who looked surprised to see me. (I don't think they had many unannounced visiting legislators.) As I waited for assistance, I noticed a sign on one of the file cabinets in a long line of file cabinets. That sign read: "Access to this file by designated employees only!!" I didn't learn much from that office.

The difficulty I experienced finding information about this land sale and the corporation involved continued to disturb me. Because I was busy with many legislative matters at that time, my legislative aide and I couldn't dig deep enough to answer my constituents' questions. However, I did do some research at the Plymouth County Registry of Deeds after my retirement, and this is what I learned: The winning bidder had been a group headed by an out-of-state realty corporation that was very difficult to trace. The person whose name was on the deed was indeed a very busy man, as evidenced by the pages of transactions with his name on them at the Registry of Deeds. He was busy buying and selling properties. His company sold the parcel at 120 Harvard Street for $150,000 to an LLC (Limited-Liability Company) that later divided the property into four buildable house lots.

There was a straw bidder (the person who makes a purchase on behalf of another person) for the group that originally put the money up for the land. This group had at first proposed turning it into a Title 40B development that would replace the original six-room house with duplexes and triplexes for a total of thirteen families. For several years, my neighbors and I fought the proposed thirteen-unit development in a succession of zoning appeal meetings during which we asked many questions. Eventually, our persistence paid off and four large homes, rather than the thirteen units, were built on that land. Each of those homes sold for $400,000. The Chisholm family, who had lived at 120 Harvard Street when I was growing up, had sold their home and the three-acre lot for $25,000 in the early 1970s. When the new buyers could no longer pay the mortgage, they abandoned the house, and the home and land lay vacant until 1998. (It bothers my sense of fairness that people of wealth seem to somehow increase their wealth through the troubles of others.)

The 40B developments are exempt from town zoning by-laws, supposedly to make more affordable housing available. Often 40B developments don't actually provide much affordable housing; instead, they are a tool used by developers to skirt local zoning laws. (Zoning is the way towns control the character of their community, and throughout our history, unfortunately, zoning has been used to exclude different races from neighborhoods.) The 40B proposal to house thirteen families in a three-acre lot on Harvard Street would have increased the street's traffic, increased public school costs, and if the property wasn't well managed, could have become a public safety expense for the town.

I don't disapprove of low-income homes or housing density in a development. Before I was a rep, I argued in a public meeting for a state group home in my neighborhood that would have served disabled people. I did this despite opposition from most of my neighbors. That group home was accepted by the town, and the residents have been good neighbors. What I don't approve of is enabling irresponsible developers to cash in on large developments under the guise of increasing affordable housing in a town.

The Whitman Armory

Other complicated local land issues occurred in our town during my years in the legislature, including one involving the Whitman Armory. In 2003, rumors circulated that the armory was going to be declared surplus property due to federal budget cuts. The armory building had potential civic use that Whitman's fire department, public works department, and police department were all interested in.

On September 3, 2003, the U.S. Department of Defense posted a list identifying nine outdated and/or redundant facilities in Massachusetts. The Whitman Armory wasn't on the list. Yet, town officials knew it had been closed since June 30, 2003, and rumor had it that the armory had been transferred to the Massachusetts Division of Capital Asset Management and Maintenance (DCAM), which is responsible for public building construction, facilities management, and real estate services for the Commonwealth. When federal property is transferred to the state for disposal, state agencies get first right of refusal. Then, if no state agency wants the property, DCAM can sell the property to the highest bidder. So why wasn't the Whitman Armory on the Department of Defense list?

The history of the armory and its surrounding land began March 15, 1922, when a Whitman resident, Margaret Hersey, donated land to the Whitman Legion Post 22 for use as an American Legion Hall. Thirty-four years later, on January 17, 1956, the Legion gave the property on which the armory was located to the Town of Whitman so it could transfer the property to the U.S. National Guard for the construction of a new armory. With the National Guard disposing of the armory, the Legion believed that the property should rightfully revert to them. They also didn't want a police station within a few hundred yards of their club. However, the American Legion lawyer back in 1956 had neglected to include a reversionary clause in the paperwork for the transfer of the land. (You do have to keep a good eye on land deals.)

I was responsible for assisting my towns that had issues with the state, and Whitman wanted the armory for the lowest price possible. (Earlier in 2003, in the town of Waltham, a private citizen had outbid the Town of Waltham at auction, paying $990,000 for the Waltham Armory. So I had my work cut out for me to prevent this from happening in Whitman.)

My first step was to stay in touch with DCAM to learn when the armory and surrounding land would be auctioned; I began by contacting a constituent and friend who worked at DCAM. He said he would keep me apprised of any movement on the armory and gave me updates when I called every couple of weeks. In the process, I learned about a state publication probably few citizens know about, called *The Central Register*. (There is a similar publication called "\ *Goods and Services*, and both are available through the Massachusetts Secretary of State.) It lists public property that is for sale and property the state is looking to buy or rent. From what I had heard, people have acquired valuable public property at very low cost.

Finally, on October 29, 2003, I received word from Congressman Stephen Lynch's office that the paperwork officially rendering the armory as surplus property was on its way to DCAM. Then the real work began: writing and filing legislation with my senate counterpart, Senator Rob Creeden from Brockton, to allow Whitman to purchase the armory for one dollar. Next, I had to request meetings with Speaker Finneran and the Ways and Means Committee chairman and his staff to secure their support for the bill. It seemed that in the spring of 2004, the State was preparing to auction the Whitman Armory but withdrew it, saying the Massachusetts Historical Society might need it for storage. Finally, on June 4, 2004, our bill proposing to sell the armory to the Town of Whitman for one dollar was signed into law. (I guess the Massachusetts Historical Society didn't want it after all.)

Throughout all of this, I was trying to make peace with the American Legion members who were still dead-set against the town's taking ownership. I tried to mediate during a meeting with a person from each side, but because of lawyer interference, this didn't work out. Two years after I left the legislature, in November 2009, the armory remained unused because of a lawsuit against the town by the American Legion. Ultimately, the Town and the Legion came to an agreement and at present, the old Whitman Armory is used by the Whitman Fire Department for drills, classes, and storage. I don't know the total amount of money spent on lawyers' fees by the U.S. government, the State of Massachusetts, the Town of Whitman, and the Whitman American Legion to resolve this issue, but I'm sure it was quite a lot. Land swaps are complicated, and it's important to keep an eye on our diminishing local open space. It seems that state and local governments don't always prioritize the needs of the people over the wants of developers. And often, only lawyers can unravel the mystery of land ownership and transfers originally created by other lawyers.

Chapter 12: Seeing Cuba with My Own Eyes

In January 2002, less than four months after the 9/11 terrorist attacks on New York City and Washington D.C., Afghanistan and Iraqi Taliban prisoners and I both arrived in Cuba.

The prisoners were sent to the U.S. Naval Base at Guantanamo Bay, where they would be tortured; and, for almost twenty years, some forty would continue to be held captive. (As I continued editing this memoir, I read in a January 10, 2020, *New York Times* article that the annual cost to house these forty prisoners is $13 million per prisoner.)

While the prisoners at Guantanamo Bay lived isolated in darkness in their cells, I went to Havana, where I stayed at the Hotel Presidente for seven days on a legislative trip co-sponsored by my colleague and officemate, Rep. Jarrett Barrios, who is of Cuban descent. We went to Cuba as part of Oxfam's ACCESSO Project that brings Americans and Cubans together for better understanding and, hopefully, for changes in current policies that keep us estranged from our neighbors living less than a hundred miles off the coast of Florida. We had obtained an exemption from the U.S. Embargo of that time that prohibited most American travel to Cuba.

Our group consisted of about twenty-five people: Jarrett Barrios, who helped organize the trip, and five legislators: Deborah Blumer, Carol Donovan, Kay Khan, Pamela Resor, and me; Johanna Weiss, a *Boston Globe* reporter; a Cuban-American administrator from Mass General Hospital, Oz Mondejar, and his partner John; a computer tech from WGBH; the president of Community Development of Boston; and several others, including political and social activists, professionals, and family members.

We brought books, paper and pens, computers, a Braille printer, basic medical supplies, and stuffed animals to give to the Cuban children. Each morning, my roommate, Carol Donovan, gave the outfit she had worn the day before to the housekeeper who cleaned our hotel room—thus improving American-Cuban relations one outfit at a time with her personal generosity. The United States Government's trade blockade with Cuba, dating back to 1961, restricted business transactions between our two countries. It also prohibited people-to-people exchanges and remittances. But that didn't keep me from leaving gratuities at restaurants and the hotel or from purchasing two amateur CDs of beautiful Cuban music that I continue enjoying to this day.

Our flights from Boston to Miami and from Miami to Cuba went smoothly. After arriving at Hotel Presidente, we had a short welcome and briefing before we received our room keys. Once in our room, Carol and I finally prepared for bed at 3:30 a.m.

We brushed our teeth with bottled water and tried, as instructed, to remember not to drink the water in Cuba because of bacteria that could wreak havoc on our digestive systems. We sparingly used a few pieces of the toilet paper we had brought from home. We had been advised to pack toilet tissues and Kleenex because of the paper shortage in Cuba. After washing, I called the front desk to request a morning wake-up call. The desk clerk responded, "Certainly, and have nice dreams!" (I still can't help but wonder what a positive environmental difference reducing the amount of paper we throw away each day would make, and what a positive international impact we could have through random acts and words of kindness.)

Seeing Havana by bus

I slept well that first night in Cuba and awoke to the sounds of dogs, chickens, and automobile horns, the smell of car exhaust fumes, and the warmth of bright sunshine coming through our open window (literally open—no screens). January 5, our first full day in Cuba, a sweater was enough to keep me warm—quite different from the layers of clothing and the frigid temperatures we had left behind in Massachusetts. Our bus took us through the streets of Havana, which were lined with stucco buildings of exquisite Spanish architecture in dire need of repair. Sharing the road with us were a few 1950s automobiles, horse-drawn carts, bicyclists, human taxis (a cart on two wheels pulled by a bicycle rider), and buses jam-packed with people.

We listened to a brief history of Cuba as we rode around the city. On the Avenue of Presidents, which had originally been planned to be lined with statues of Cuban presidents, there was only one Cuban president, Jose Miguel Gomez (1909-1913), along with the Cuban Revolutionary hero, Che Guevara, and a few presidents from other Latin American countries. During this trip I learned and appreciated more clearly Cuba's relationship with our country.

After the Spanish American War (1898-1902), part of our agreement with Spain had made Cuba (formerly under Spanish control) a protectorate of the United States. Under this agreement, the U.S. supported the Cuban military dictatorship of President Batista. This gave U.S. companies and the American government domination over Cuban agriculture, industry, and trade. The majority of Cubans lived in poverty and the U.S. Mafia took advantage of this to promote the sale of illegal drugs and prostitution in Cuba. In 1959, Fidel Castro led the Cuban Revolution that removed Batista, and he formed another military dictatorship—this time putting all U.S. properties under Cuban governance. The United States retaliated with an embargo against Cuba in 1960 that was still in force during our visit. (Because of our embargo, Castro allied Cuba with Communist Russia/ Soviet Union. And Russia, seeking a foothold in the Western hemisphere, was happy to sell Cuba fuel and other economic necessities.)

We rode through the Miramar section of Havana, which had been the very wealthy section of the city until the exodus during the Revolution in 1959-1962. These once elegant homes with beautifully landscaped gardens and lawns are now government property used at the whim of state officials. From what we saw that morning, life in Cuba was frozen in time and looked mostly as it had in 1962 at the beginning of Fidel Castro's dictatorship and the American boycott and embargo.

Each day and every night, we experienced a different aspect of Cuban life. During a visit to the Cuban National Library, we toured the children's section of the library. It was smaller than any of the elementary school libraries in my hometown of Whitman. There, we saw university students studying from books, most of which had been printed before 1959. Students used recycled paper for their notes and were very careful about rationing their paper supply. The country was, no doubt, still recovering from the "special period" of total economic collapse—from 1990 through 2000, when Cuba's main importer/exporter, the Soviet Union, dissolved. (Living through the COVID-19 pandemic's losses in human life and the worst job losses since the Great Depression, and the January 6, 2021 insurrection to stop our government from functioning, I am thankful for our Democracy even with its imperfections!)

Government restrictions in Cuba in 2002 limited book borrowing according to a citizen's level of education. A university degree entitled one to borrow any book. Others could apply for special permission to read books beyond their education level. Not all the books we had brought with us would be made available to the Cuban people, since every book was censored by government officials before being placed on library shelves. Scarce electrical power also limited library use to daylight hours. (How fortunate we Americans are with our freedom to obtain uncensored information, freedom to express our opinions, and access to electricity and other utilities that we so often take for granted.)

Visiting Cuban schools, medical facilities, and dental offices

Another day, we visited an elementary school for deaf and blind children. The elementary students performed a story from native Cuban folklore as their teacher narrated the story. As I watched these beautiful, innocent children, tears filled my eyes just as they had when I had watched my own children participate in school performances.

Despite differences in languages, abilities, and opposing governments, we were all one in our love of children and the joyful music.

As in the United States, education in Cuba is mandatory until
age sixteen. The Cuban students had longer school days than American students. They enjoyed classes in art, music, drama, and physical
education daily along with their math, science, history, and language
courses. Education was a priority and people were very well trained
for whatever profession they were determined (by tests) to be capable
of studying for. Sadly, many Cubans trained as teachers, psycholo-
gists, and other professionals were working as taxi drivers, bus
drivers, and waitresses because they made more money in the tourism
industry than the seven to ten dollars a week they would have earned
in their professions.

I was especially interested in our visits to a doctor's office, a
hospital, and the Catholic Charities Office because of my involvement back home on the Massachusetts Joint Committee on Health
Care. We visited a typical hospital and saw patients with IVs hang-
ing from rusted, paint-flaked poles, and an ER with patients in one
large room accompanied by family members sitting in old aluminum
lawn chairs. Many bathrooms didn't have running water. Nurses
and doctors reused syringes and rubber gloves because of the shortage of medical supplies. In medicine, as in other aspects of their
lives, Cubans made up for what they lacked in resources with their
exceptional education, training, and dedication. Nurses worked hard
to prevent infections and bed sores, and they kept patients hydrated
and watched over them carefully. (Back in Massachusetts, I had been
working to pass legislation for nurse safe-staffing ratios. Year after
year, American nurses have stressed the importance of having time
to take care of these preventative measures.) When we visited the
children's ward, we brought teddy bears for the patients. A young
blind boy, probably six years old, who had had surgery to remove a
third eye from the top of his head, received one of our teddy bears.
His response was, "Because of what you have done for me, I know

there is a God."

Cuba had one dentist for every thousand people, and each person was entitled to a free dental check-up every six months. In the U.S., oral health care is not generally covered by our health insurance, and we must buy separate dental insurance that still doesn't cover complicated procedures. In some rural places in the U.S., people with extreme dental pain travel for a day and wait in long lines to find a dentist who will treat them.

In Cuba, the ratio of medical doctors to citizens was one for every 200 citizens, and Cuban doctors were available twenty-four hours a day, seven days a week. This was in contrast to the doctor shortage looming today in the U.S. Most Cuban doctors are trained in natural medicine and use nutrition, herbal remedies, acupuncture, massage, and other traditional modalities to enable the body to heal itself. Back in Massachusetts, as the sponsor of a bill to license naturopathic doctors, I was a member of the Special Commission on Complementary and Alternative Medical Practices. Medical societies and pharmaceutical companies had worked hard to keep these alternative practices on the fringe—they thought of their practitioners as quacks. Throughout my years in the legislature I sponsored legislation to license naturopathic doctors who had eight years of education, passed board of registration exams, and participated in internships alongside traditional medical doctors because I believed in the holistic approach to health care. The licensure bill, after more than twenty years of re-files, finally became law in 2017.

In Cuba, prescription medications as we know them today are scarce and available mostly from donations such as ours through Catholic Charities. The priest at Catholic Charities showed us how drugs were dispensed from shoe boxes stored in a closet in his office. With the billions of dollars spent on health care and billions more spent advertising prescription drugs in America, our average life expectancy is no better than Cuban life expectancy. According to United Nations compiled statistics, America's 2018 life expectancy was 78.81 years, while our per capita healthcare expense was $10,637 (www.macrotrends.net). In that same year, Cuba's life expectancy was 78.79 years at a per capita expense of $987. With our life expectancy only three one-hundredths of a year better than Cuba's, I believe people in both countries would be healthier and enjoy a longer life with loved ones if we shared knowledge and resources.

Speaking through translators, the Cuban people we met told us they wanted to see the United States and Cuba come together as mutually beneficial neighbors. We are located less than one hundred miles from each other, and I believe all our lives would be enriched through renewed friendly relationships. Cuban parents told us that America is a model of hope for the better life they want for their children. The authoritarian dictatorships they have lived under have limited their chances of fulfilling their dreams. It is my dream that more Americans will engage in our democratic process so our country will better live up to the values our Declaration of Independence espouses, that "All men are created equal and are endowed by their Creator with the unalienable rights of life, liberty, and the pursuit of happiness." Then we can be a true model of hope for the suppressed around the world.

The average Cuban desires a peaceful life enjoyed with family and friends. During my ten years in the Massachusetts House of Representatives, these were the same values I heard expressed when I had the opportunity to meet people who came to the State House on economic, cultural, social, and political visits from Brazil, Armenia, Ireland, developing African countries, China, Japan, Israel, and all parts of the United States. I believe these are the values of people throughout the world.

Reflections on our "enemies"

Staying a mere two-hour drive from the prison yards of the 9/11 Al-qaeda terrorists on the small island of Cuba during my 2002 visit didn't make me nervous. What has made me nervous is our inhumane treatment of the Guantanamo prisoners held all these years without a trial and our pre-emptive war with Iraq, based on lies about their weapons of mass destruction. These have surely motivated more terrorists and more violence against America. Just as Fidel Castro blamed many of Cuba's problems on the 1960 U.S. embargo against Cuba, leaders of other countries can and do cite our actions in their propaganda against us.

Upon returning home from Cuba in January 2002, I listened in disbelief as President George W. Bush named Iran, Iraq, and North Korea the "axis of evil" in his State of the Union speech. Our next generation was being taught that these people were our "enemies" just as I had been taught that Cuba was an enemy.

After 9/11

After 9/11, the United States spent a whopping $6.4 trillion dollars to fight Wars on Terror ("Post 9/11 U.S. Wars on Terror," Pardee School of Global Affairs, Boston University, Nov. 19, 2019) which also took hundreds of thousands of lives and destroyed and then re-built infrastructure. I wonder what would have happened if, instead of financing wars, we had used those trillions of dollars to feed hungry children, to bring water to drought-ravaged regions of the world, to repair dangerously aging infrastructure such as the failed New Orleans levees during Hurricane Katrina, and to provide better health care and education to all in our country. (Americans, as President Eisenhower warned in 1961, must be vigilant in monitoring the military-industrial complex.)

Attending support gatherings for families of the more than 300 Massachusetts 9/11 victims, I got to meet families and hear their varied responses to their tragic losses. One of these people was my constituent and friend Christie Coombs, the widow of Jeffrey Coombs who was killed on Flight 11, which departed from Logan Airport that fateful morning and crashed into the Twin Towers in New York. The Coombs family, like many of the victims' families, turned their sorrow into efforts to benefit others. The Jeffrey Coombs

Memorial Foundation has raised more than a million dollars to address the needs of Abington children.

Other local 9/11 widows included Susan Retik and Patti Quigley. They used money they received from their husbands' life insurance policies and public donations to create and support a foundation to assist the one million civil war widows in Afghanistan. Their story is told in an award-winning documentary, Beyond Belief, produced by Beth Murphy. Meeting with some of the Afghani widows, Patti and Susan learned that women in Afghanistan have the same core values women and men in the United States hold dear. In fact, parents all over the world have these same core values; they want health, education, and happiness for their children and their family members.

Today, I think back on my visit to Cuba and my many meetings with people from all world regions and walks of life. Those encounters convince me that we are all neighbors who can solve our differences in ways that will enable us to be enriched by our beautiful diversity and flourish in our mutual pursuit of a better life for our children.

Chapter 13: "Ordinary Working Stiffs" and Campaign Finance Reform

The man standing before me was extremely upset. I had expressed my disappointment with the 2002 statewide vote reversing the 1998 Massachusetts Clean Election Ballot Initiative. His perspective was: "I don't want some ordinary working stiff representing me in the State House!"

From his words and tone, I understood that his opinion was quite different from mine. He and I were in the parking lot of Holy Ghost Church, Whitman, after a 9 a.m. daily Mass, and he had asked, "Well, what's new at the State House?" After my election, I found that no matter where I was, people wanted to discuss politics, and this gentleman gave me an earful about his opposition to campaign finance reform. He didn't see any problem with the candidacies of the more financially well-to-do, and, as he said, "more educated," having a campaign advantage over the average "working stiff." I bit my tongue as I thought about all those "working stiffs" who labor, sweat, and work ungodly hours under dangerous conditions to create the wealth and profits that companies and shareholders enjoy.

I believed then and still do that those who achieve economic success do not have an exclusive hold on intelligence and leadership. Good governing is not based on improving profits and the Gross National Product; it's about improving the quality of life for everyone in our generation and all those who will follow us. The campaign finance reforms would also have created a level playing field for the opponents of the career politicians who amass large "war chests" of campaign contributions. I had a lot more I wanted to say, but the issue was complicated, and I didn't think the church parking lot was the place for a heated debate. Looking back, I think the church parking lot actually was the right place for debates!

The Clean Elections Ballot Initiative

In the 1998 election, sixty-six percent of Massachusetts voters had passed the Campaign Finance Reform ballot initiative, sponsored by Common Cause, a non-profit political watchdog. Having the League of Women Voters endorse this move gave me confidence and hope! The reform measure, referred to as the "Clean Elections Ballot Initiative" question, advocated for public financing of state campaigns for candidates who agreed to contribution limits, spending limits, and the collection of qualifying contributions from those who signed a candidate's nomination papers. This favorable vote had also created a campaign finance dollar donation check-off on Massachusetts tax return forms. (I was happy to check this box each time I filed my taxes.) Included in the initiative was a way to ensure that only legitimate candidates could access public campaign funding. A state representative, for example, would need to have at least 150 or 200 nomination-paper signers contribute between five and one hundred dollars each, to prove credibility in order to qualify for public campaign funding.

Passage of the Clean Elections Ballot Initiative was due to the hard work of volunteers around the state who gave their time, energy, and determination to this, in my opinion, very important cause. (To learn more about the ballot initiative process, see Appendix 10.) As a Massachusetts resident, you may have been asked to sign this or other initiative petitions such as the safe nurse staffing petition that I signed recently.

Following the overwhelming vote in favor of the Clean Elections Ballot Initiative, Beacon Hill was a hive of activity as we tried to ensure the funding for it. Forty-four strong supporters out of the 200-member legislature supported the bill, moving it forward. I was one of them because I believed campaign expenditures in state and federal elections were and continue to be out of control. Proponents attempted to persuade the legislature to fund this program at ten million dollars for public financing of future campaigns. Ten million dollars equaled six one-hundredths of one percent of the state budget, and it made sense that six one-hundredths of a percent of our budget was a good investment in restoring democracy for our citizens by reducing the amount of special-interest money influencing our political system and our government.

Because only the legislature could budget money, and because the Speaker opposed campaign finance reform, no money was appropriated for the new initiative. As a result, Senator Warren Tolman (D-Watertown), who had been a staunch supporter of campaign finance reform, filed a suit against the State for the funding in case the initiative won its necessary second vote in 2002.

I learned during my years on Beacon Hill that the Commonwealth could have wonderful policies and programs, but if no funding existed for implementation, services, or enforcement, all was for naught! I also learned that House and Senate leadership had the power to block funding for the Clean Elections ballot initiative that sixty-six percent of the people who voted in 1998 had supported.

The 2002 voter rejection of the Clean Election Initiative was extremely disheartening to me and to all who worked so hard to achieve its passage in 1998. I believe it was also disappointing to most of my constituents, because during each of my campaigns for re-election I had heard increasing election cynicism from voters. Over and over again, they told me campaigns were too long, too much money was spent on media ads, there was too much mudslinging, and it was becoming more and more difficult to know which candidates were telling the truth. I felt, and still believe, that we should shorten campaign seasons to a maximum of six months. (Other countries have limits on the length of campaigns.)

The need for limits on campaign spending

In my opinion, all candidates on the ballot should receive the same amount of media coverage and a limited amount of campaign funding.

The average voter often does not have the time or energy to

thoroughly research candidates' backgrounds and all stands on issues. In most Massachusetts families, both spouses work, and sometimes they work more than one job to pay their bills. Network media tell us about automobile accidents, murders, fires, dog bites, and the weather—with little information that could help us make good political decisions. Families pay hundreds of dollars each year for cable TV that initially promised to be commercial-free. Yet, year after year we see more commercials, including numerous campaign ads aired between each six-minute news segment! In the 2020 presidential election, close to $7 billion was spent nation-wide on network and cable TV ads. This gives political incumbents with war chests an advantage over candidates who must spend a lot of time and energy fundraising. From what I have experienced, many news outlets are more concerned with making money than with providing citizens with information they need to vote responsibly. (Before 1970, federal communications laws required networks to provide certain amounts of national and international reporting, but that's a whole different story.) (For news, I recommend the PBS World News which airs from 6 to 7 p.m., EST, Monday-Friday, on Channel 2, along with balanced local newspapers so you learn all sides of issues.)

A big-money defeat for the clean election law

After the 2002 state election, it was disclosed that Speaker Finneran and special interest groups worked to defeat the Clean Elections ballot initiative of 1998, despite the initiative's intent to remove some of the moneyed influence on Massachusetts government. They spent $1.5 million on TV, radio, and print propaganda opposing campaign finance reform. Because the law regulating the reporting of campaign funding for initiative petitions allowed report filings as late as 5 p.m. on Election Day, voters could not and did not know that the barrage of negative ads against the Clean Election Law was primarily funded by powerful corporate donors whose businesses were directly affected by government policies and contracts. These expensive ads were full of propaganda that successfully convinced Massachusetts voters that campaign finance reform was not in their best interests. Thus, the citizen-initiated reforms that two-thirds of Massachusetts voters had supported in 1998 was soundly defeated in 2002.

The important message here is not so much that we should be enraged with Speaker Finneran and the corporations that he worked with to defeat this initiative. We should instead be working to understand how too much power and money have come to control much of government not only in Massachusetts but throughout the country. We need to volunteer and vote for candidates who will work to reform campaigns, especially their financing. Many good candidates exist, some of them wealthy like Mitt Romney and Charlie Baker, and some of them—like Deval Patrick, Warren Tolman, and me— "ordinary working stiffs." We need women and men who will have the courage and ethics to lead us to a more just, more honest, and more peaceful society. A level campaign finance playing field would get us much closer to that goal.

Chapter 14: Life and Death Issues, and the Gay Marriage Vote

Back in 1995, when my husband Bob Teahan told me that I'd like being a state rep because I could make a difference in people's lives, I had no idea about the magnitude of the impact my votes would have. While I wanted to make more of an impact on people's lives, I have never regretted the time I gave trying to make a positive difference.

In February 2004, during my fourth term in the legislature, I found myself in the midst of what I believe was the most important vote of the century: the vote to allow gay marriage. Let me set the context.

Massachusetts had recovered from the economic recession of the early 1990s and the 2001 financial downturn. The legislature had narrowly maintained its stand against the death penalty (thanks to Rep. John Slattery's tie-breaking vote) in spite of the aggressive push by Governor Cellucci and the Republicans to reinstate the death penalty after the kidnapping and murder of a ten-year-old named Jeffrey Curley. The world had survived the great Millennium Scare concerning the potential for world-wide chaos as clocks and calendars and our computerized world turned the page from the 1900s and entered the year 2000.

I will never forget the devastating 9/11 terrorist attack and the loss of 300 people from Massachusetts, including my constituents Jeff Coombs, a young father of three from Abington who died on Flight 11, and Craig Miller, an East Bridgewater native, father of four sons and a master special officer with the U.S. Secret Service. I rode the train to Boston that day and knew nothing about the attack until I reached my State House office where the television was showing live coverage from New York. In all, 3,000 people died in the attacks on New York's Twin Towers, the Pentagon, and in Shanksville, Pennsylvania, and there were unknown hundreds who eventually suffered from PTSD, lung problems, cancers, and many other injuries.

In Gardner Auditorium in the Massachusetts State House, I had spoken at hearings attended by Cardinal Bernard Law on doctor-assisted suicide bills, and I had been a member of a special study on End of Life needs and care. (When a reporter asked if my votes followed Cardinal Law's lead, my response was, "when I agreed with him.") I worked on issues involving children in foster care, served on a special commission on adoption and went to D.C. to receive the 2003 Congressional Angels in Adoption Award aimed at raising awareness about the millions of orphans around the world in need of permanent, safe, and loving families. Each of the ten years I served in the House of Representatives was full of extremely serious issues.

But it was the 2004 vote on gay marriage that had my telephone ringing off the hook, my mailbox full of letters, and my computer screen overflowing with email messages.

This vote came after decades of struggles by the gay and lesbian community to gain the recognition and equal rights afforded other people in the Commonwealth. Because of past legislative inaction on bills to legalize gay marriage, the advocacy group Gay and Lesbian Legal Advocates and Defenders (GLAD), supported seven gay couples who brought their case (named Goodridge et al. v. Department of Public Health) to the Massachusetts Supreme Court. On November 18, 2003, the Court ruled four to three that gay couples should have the same rights that the Massachusetts Constitution guarantees to all, including the right to obtain a marriage license and marry. The Court put a 180-day stay on their decision to give the Legislature time to take action on the case. It was during this time that I was involved with an issue of historic importance.

After the decision on the Goodridge case, Governor Mitt Romney filed an amendment (H.3190 An Act to Amend the Constitution Relative to the Affirmation of Marriage) to define marriage as between a man and a woman, and this was what started the barrage of calls to my office. My very loving and competent aide Jennifer patiently and politely recorded the content of each call, keeping a tally of whether a caller was for or against H.3190. Several priests and ministers from my district called and met with me to ask me to vote for this amendment to the Massachusetts Constitution and thus to define marriage as a union of one man and one woman.

I was a Catholic who had been elected as a Pro-Life Democrat because I believed (and still do) that every life is precious, and that we had a responsibility to do our best to ensure that every child had the love, food, and education needed to survive and thrive in life. I had been a member of Holy Ghost Catholic Church all my life. As a young girl, I had memorized my catechism lessons so well that I usually won prizes for being the most prepared in my group. During the Children's Mass, the nuns would choose me to lead everyone to the Communion rail because I was so attentive and knew the Mass sequence by heart. As a Girl Scout, I received the highest Catholic Scout Award, the Marian Medal. I had been the Catholic Youth Organization (CYO) vice president during my high school years. In the 1980s, I had coordinated religious education at Holy Ghost Parish with my Aunt Ann Tonello and became a Eucharistic Minister. In the 1990s, I served on the Parish Council, wrote articles for our weekly parish newsletter, helped write the mission statement and spiritual history of the parish, and continued as a Eucharistic Minister. During the 2000s, I participated in adoration of the Eucharist every Tuesday morning from 6 to7 a.m. and continued to serve on the parish council. My faith, passed on to me through my parents' words and actions, was a huge part of my life, and it meant a lot to me. Naturally, many of my Catholic supporters expected me to support the Constitutional Amendment to Define Marriage.

The struggle between tradition and heart

I was deeply torn between following my church and following my heart, which had been nurtured and inspired by my church. As a child, I had never accepted the Catholic Church's concept of limbo, a place where the souls of innocent, unbaptized babies went because they were not cleansed of Original Sin. I couldn't imagine a God of love who "called each by name before we were born" would discriminate against children who died without being baptized. In 2004, I didn't believe a God of love would discriminate against children born with a sexual preference different from mine.

Research had shown that humans are born with, rather than develop, their sexual preferences. My god-daughter was gay, I had gay cousins, and several friends were gay. The dentist who served with me on the Special Commission on Oral Health, Dr. Rob Compton, along with his partner David Wilson, were among the lead plaintiffs in the Massachusetts Supreme Court Case that brought the gay marriage issue to a head. I had grown to respect and admire Rob during our work on oral health. He was a Vietnam veteran and worked diligently to improve oral health for the citizens of Massachusetts. I had come to believe that changing the Massachusetts Constitution with this amendment would render gays and lesbians second class citizens, and my religious and moral beliefs convinced me that a loving God would not want this.

The final tally of correspondence from my district was approximately two to one in favor of defining marriage as the union of one man and one woman. Although I strongly believed that defining marriage as between one man and one woman in the Constitution was wrong, I found it very difficult to vote in opposition to the views of many of my constituents. I understood where they were coming from. Marriage had traditionally been between a man and a woman, and it had only been a matter of a few decades since gays and lesbians had begun to more openly present their lifestyles to families and friends. In Whitman and so many other places, families had disowned their own gay children or hid the truth about them even after they died. "I'm not telling you how to vote, but do you really want to take a vote that is going to seriously jeopardize your re-election?" asked my good friend George Lynch. Did I want to sacrifice the opportunity to serve in the legislature, to continue fighting for all the issues that I had championed over the past six years: oral health, the environment, education, and children's issues? No other representative in Plymouth County was voting against Governor Romney's amendment, and I believed that if I did, I would be targeted by conservatives in the September primary and November election.

In my heart this was a human rights issue, and I could not sit back and allow discrimination against a group of innocent people. When asked by colleagues in favor of gay marriage to help defeat Governor Romney's amendment during our Constitutional Convention, I had to join them and stand up for human rights! I attended strategy planning sessions. I was responsible for knowing how five of my colleagues would vote on various roll calls and for trying to move or keep them in favor of marriage equality. There was a lot to keep track of because at one point the marriage equality group agreed to a vote that wasn't in favor of gay marriage in order to ensure a future vote for marriage equality. This vote was a strategy vote to put us in the majority to define marriage and, thus, enable us to make a motion to reconsider the vote (according to Parliamentary Procedures).

During the Constitutional Convention, we wore beepers and reported to Room 328 in the members' lounge, just outside the Chamber, to check our progress and update our plans. When the debate started in the Chamber, members took the podium and gave heartfelt speeches about their stands on gay marriage. Throughout the halls of the State House and overflowing to the front of the building and across Beacon Street into the Boston Common, peaceful demonstrators for both sides marched, chanted, prayed, sang, and waited throughout the day and into the night for the final vote.

Speaking for gay marriage

At ten minutes to midnight on February 12, 2004, Senate President Robert Travaligni recognized me, and I took the floor. "Mr. President and Members of the Legislature, it is very fitting that I speak to you about marriage tonight because February 12 is my wedding anniversary. In just a few minutes, my late husband Bob Teahan and I would have been married for thirty-three years. Bob and I were not your average couple. He was fifty years old, and I was twenty-four when we married in 1971. Many people saw our relationship as unnatural. Yet, we had a great marriage. We supported each other in ways that allowed us both to grow and flourish, and our love grew with each passing year. We had four wonderful children, my step-daughters Anne and Jeanie, and our two sons Bobby and John, whom we loved unconditionally, nurtured to the best of our ability, and proudly saw grow into four caring, good citizens.

"Opponents to gay marriage say that children growing up in a family without both a mother and a father will lack male and female role models and be at a disadvantage. Bob's father died when he was eight years old. His mother taught school to support the family and raised three children on her own. Her daughter Mary became a stewardess—flight attendant, in today's parlance—for American Airlines and had her pilot's license. Her son Ed served as a marine in World War II and later rose to the rank of colonel in the Massachusetts State Police. And her son Bob served in Germany in World War II, fought in the Battle of the Bulge and was a Massachusetts State Representative from 1974 to 1978. He devoted his life to helping young people, especially boys, as a high school physical education teacher, athletic director, and high school and semi-pro football coach. Bob voted in favor of gay rights when he served in the legislature back in the 1970s. Families are unique and succeed according to the commitment, understanding, sacrifice, hard work, and love parents share with their children. For these reasons, and because I believe our Constitution should be amended only to extend, rather than exclude, rights to certain groups, I will vote against amending the Massachusetts Constitution to define marriage, and I urge my colleagues to do likewise."

I was the last person to speak before the Senate President introduced an amendment that Speaker Finneran and he had devised to add to the main amendment as a compromise, and he called for the vote. This compromise created civil unions for gay and lesbian couples and still defined marriage as between a man and a woman. The vote was 121 to 77 in favor of the compromise—still, I felt, a discriminatory amendment to our Massachusetts Constitution.

Opponents of gay marriage had two years of work ahead of them to define marriage as between a man and a woman in the Massachusetts Constitution. In order to amend the Constitution in this way, it would take another favorable vote of the legislature at another Constitutional Convention, followed by a referendum vote by the voters, to finalize this modification to our Constitution. Those of us fighting a change to the Constitution could not let our guard down because there were still three months before May 17, 2004, the date when gay marriages would be legal as declared in the Massachusetts Supreme Court's Goodridge Decision.

Personal repercussions from a vote

There were consequences to my vote in favor of gay marriage. One email written in all capital letters read, "How do you call yourself a Catholic? I hope that you will remember to cross your fingers when you go to receive Communion because you are such a hypocrite."

I can remember vividly my experience at the 4 p.m. Mass on the Saturday before Mother's Day 2004. I sat alone in the pew, a few feet from the visiting priest while he delivered his sermon in the center of the church. He told the parishioners how important it was for them to contact "Representative Kathleen Teahan who claimed to be a Catholic," to let her know that they wanted to be able to vote on a referendum on whether to include a definition of marriage in the state constitution. If they didn't stand up for the protection of marriage, he said, they'd have to "answer to their Maker on Judgment Day." My heart pounded and my face flushed as I numbly participated in the remainder of the Mass in the very parish where I had found peace, love, and joy for fifty-four years.

At the conclusion of the Mass, Barry Geraghty, a very tall

police officer with a heart bigger than his height, came to my seat and said, "No one is going to bother you," as he escorted me to the back of the church. Bill, a man with special needs who often bagged my groceries at Stop & Shop, said, "I didn't like what that priest said." People hugged me and told me how upset they were with the priest's personal reference to me during a Mass. John Hopkins, a lector during that Mass and a devout Catholic, told the priest how upset he and many others were with his homily.

A few weeks later, during the sign of peace at Sunday Mass, a mother told her children not to shake my hand because I was an evil person. That made me wonder what other situations I might face when I attended Mass in the future.

One Tuesday at 6 a.m. as I entered the lower church for my weekly Hour of Adoration, my eyes were drawn to a pile of Catholic Voter Guides on the table at the back of the church. The guides stated that a serious Catholic would vote *only* for people who fell in line with Catholic teachings and traditions. I brought one of these booklets to the rectory to ask my pastor about them. I wanted to learn whether he had sanctioned the booklets or whether an individual parishioner had anonymously left them in the church. An elderly priest in the parish took the booklet, but I never heard from the pastor. He may have had the same questions about the Church's position about gay marriage that I had. Even though, when celebrating a Mass I attended at my parish, Cardinal Law repeatedly stressed that the Catholic Church didn't provide options for "cafeteria" Catholics, I knew wonderful priests, nuns, and lay persons who had beliefs similar to mine.

The day after the final gay marriage debate, my aide Jennifer gave me two folders, thick with email responses to my votes. The folder of negative reactions contained very harsh words from a Catholic in Abington who had voted for me because of my pro-life stand. In the positive response folder was a full page email from a stranger in Worcester, Massachusetts, who wrote, "When I was about eight, a little friend came over to tell me that he could not play with me anymore because his mother said I was not normal like other little boys. I didn't understand what that meant, but when I went to junior high and got my first beating for being different, I soon found out what "not normal" meant. My mother tried to intervene, but I soon got the name "Mama's Boy," and the beatings became worse and more frequent. I was punched in the stomach and face, spit at, and forced to perform sex acts on the bullies. The teacher told my mother that I got what I deserved; I walked like a girl and had a high-pitched voice. At fifteen, I told God I was sorry but I just could not take it anymore, and I tried to kill myself with sleeping pills. Obviously, I didn't die. When the vote came in last night, I became closer to being normal. From the bottom of my heart, I thank you for making such a difficult vote in the State House. Today, for the first time in fifty-five years I feel NORMAL! God Bless you and Happy Anniversary. Your husband and you will be in my prayers ALWAYS!"

A few weeks after the gay marriage vote, I received a call from John Henning, a young lawyer from California who, with his friend Mike Roth, was making a documentary about the gay marriage issue. John asked if I would do an interview on film about my vote and my experiences related to gay marriage and whether he could tape me while door-knocking in my district during the upcoming campaign. I agreed. I chose a working family neighborhood with about twenty-five homes off of Route 139 in Abington. Mike Roth followed me with his camera, and I was amazed at the warm welcomes and positive responses I received as I asked constituents for their votes. One woman told me how proud she was to have a person of courage for her representative and asked her teenagers to come to their front door to meet me.

Serving in the Massachusetts House of Representatives for ten years was the opportunity of a lifetime. Every day was different and challenging, and I remember them all fondly. I remember the thrill of walking on the worn marble stairs in the State House where thousands of my legislative predecessors had walked since 1898. I remember my panic when I thought I was locked alone inside the Paulist Center Chapel (located one hundred yards down Park Street from the State House). I had gone there to have a quiet place to gather my thoughts and words before a late-night death penalty debate. (I eventually found a custodian who let me out.) I was thrilled when Rep. Gloria Fox (D-Roxbury), a strong Black colleague, called me "sister" when I was supporting an issue in her district. I cried tears of sorrow and anger when I listened to adult men tell how their molestation by Catholic priests was ignored. I blushed with embarrassment when Mayor Jack Yunits asked if I wanted to keep the pink curler in my hair as I entered the Enterprise Building in Brockton for a radio interview. I felt a warm comradery with female NRA members during the National Rifle Association Convention I attended in Arizona as a substitute for Rep. Susan Pope (R-Wayland). (Susan's high school constituent won an NRA scholarship, but she would not receive the prize without being accompanied at the convention by a legislator.) And yes, I felt pride when that Abington mother praised me for my gay marriage vote. When I left the legislature, I was thankful for the opportunity to serve the people of Massachusetts. The memory goes on and so does my desire to help others.

I am so thankful that Bob encouraged me to enter politics. Now it is my dream that courageous, caring people, especially women, will run for elected office.

Chapter 15: Reflections on Going Forward— The Way I See Things Today

I. Today, I see that money is having too powerful an influence on government.

Congress and state legislatures are not functioning for the American people because of the severe bipartisan divides caused by money and power that make re-elections predominate over doing what's best for the people. It's complicated. Because getting elected is important, and campaigns can be extremely expensive, politicians depend on donations of big-money individuals and corporations to win their elections. It is only human that politicians listen more closely and become more influenced by the people who financially support their campaigns.

Think back to the money spent on the 2008 and 2012 national election campaigns, not to mention the 2016 and 2020 campaigns. Nearly six billion dollars was spent on the 2008 presidential and congressional campaigns, according to the Center for Responsive Politics and Robert Kaiser writing in *The Washington Post*, September 2009. Seven billion dollars was spent in the 2012 elections, according to the Federal Elections Commission February 2013 report. Presidential and congressional campaign spending in 2016 was $7.2 billion, and it doubled in 2020 to nearly $14 billion. (opensecrets.org; Center for Responsive Politics, October 26, 2020) How many people world-wide would that money have saved from starvation?

Having enough financial support to defend against an opponent's negative campaigning and to present your own clear message to voters is more and more challenging, especially after the U.S. Supreme Court's 2010 Citizens United decision in favor of unlimited campaign contributions from corporations, associations, and labor unions. With this outside money, groups can often control election results by feeding voters misinformation about the candidates they oppose. Oil industries donated over $5 million to California candidates in the 2006 election. Our government continues to subsidize oil companies. Even though oil profits decreased with the COVID pandemic and other factors, Exxon Mobile's 2020 revenue was $249 billion with a loss of $20 billion, and Chevron's was $135 billion with a loss of $5.5 billion; they both still made money. (See www. statista.com, June 9, 2020, "2020 Ranking of U.S. Oil and Gas Companies," by N. Sonnichsen, and "Oil Company Losses in 2021 were Staggering," *The Washington Post*, by Will England, February 4, 2021.)

Our United States fiscal year 2020 budget totaled $6.6 trillion dollars. Sixty percent of this was mandatory spending for Social Security, Medicare, and Medicaid. Forty percent was for discretionary spending, which showed a large increase in defense spending and large cuts to funds for domestic needs such as health, education, agriculture, the environment, state aid, and international security. ("FY 2020 Fact Sheet: U.S. Spending," Women's Actions for New Directions (WAND), Washington, D.C.)

Earmarks in legislation and budgets can be a way of rewarding donors by funding their projects. Other earmarks, with support from the speaker of the house or the senate president, direct funds to specific businesses or local funding in a legislator's district. These earmarks help candidates help their districts, but they most often take money away from other more vital projects. Many times I heard from workers and leaders in state agencies and departments—such as for state parks, revenue, children and families, division of insurance, and public health—that eliminating budget earmarks would enable government to address needs that would improve the quality and efficiency of services provided for our citizens. An example of an earmark from 2006, was the $47 billion in defense contracts earmarked in federal budgeting that year; contributions to federal candidates from defense earmark recipients totaled $1.4 billion in 2006. In FY'08, the largest defense industry earmark that year was $588 million to accelerate production of U.S. Navy submarines, and it was inserted against U.S. Navy requests. "In a report to Congress, the Navy said boosting the production of submarines would disrupt its overall shipbuilding plan by shifting [funding] from other important programs." (The Hill, February 13, 2007)

Another problem with our present way of financing campaigns is the challenge of running against opponents who have almost limitless resources. There is presently no limit on the amount of money a candidate can contribute to her/his own campaign. Also, incumbents who can amass millions of dollars in their campaign war chests have a great advantage over political newcomers who must expend precious campaign time raising funds for a campaign. Amounts in these war chests grow yearly from donations from special interest groups that want easy access to politicians, the very people who determine the direction of government policies and where our billions of tax dollars will go.

Besides influencing what issues are addressed and how they are addressed, the money influence in our government discourages people from voting when they see their vote as insignificant against millions of special-interest dollars spent on political campaigns.

So what can we do about money in politics?

We can start by expecting politicians to see each other not just as Democrats or Republicans but as Americans. We can expect politicians to listen carefully and respectfully to people's opinions that are different from theirs. We can expect politicians who will stand up to House and Senate leadership and vote for the common good! We can all see compromise as the way our Democracy moves forward toward that more perfect Union.

We can learn about candidates and then volunteer for and vote for candidates who will work to take the money out of politics and support transparency in government at all levels. We can demand voting laws that guarantee easy and accessible voting for all.

We can strengthen our individual voices by contacting elected officials. Recently, I joined Network (a progressive Catholic social justice lobby group formed by Sister Simone Campbell), that sends texts about calls to make when important social justice issues are at stake and connects you, with a click on your phone, to your federal rep and senators.) I also keep handy a contact list of my Massachusetts rep and senator to save time when I want to request their support on an issue. Clear and concise emails and phone calls from voters get attention. Our voices strengthen when we join unions and support unions. Together, we have powerful voices. For more strength, we can work to unite various activist groups—environmentalists, fighters for racial justice, social justice advocates, trade and labor unions—to support policies for the common good. (Exemplifying this type of merging: Sunrise Boston, Act On Mass, Mijente Boston, and the Indivisible Mass Coalition have joined together to make the Massachusetts State House more transparent and accessible to people of the Commonwealth.)

II. Today in Massachusetts and the United States, I see political leaders who wield too much power.

Powerful leaders in the Massachusetts Legislature and in Congress determine the amount of staff each representative or senator has and who chairs committees or holds other leadership positions and receives the additional compensation for those positions. When special commissions are formed to actually research and analyze issues, such as licensing naturopathic doctors, the speaker or senate president determines what special interests will be represented and the amount of power various participants will wield in the committee decision-making. During my decade in the Massachusetts Legislature, 1997-2007, the speaker pretty much controlled the inner workings of the legislative process including committee actions, which bills and budget items passed, office location and space, and the location of parking spaces. This situation is very similar in the U.S. Senate!

During my years in the legislature, members outside the inner leadership circle were often, and still are, left out of deliberations and decision making. I remember vividly an incident when I was at the rostrum in the House Chamber wanting to participate in a discussion with the speaker and others about health care. Two female reps in leadership told me to sit down, which I did not do. Other than that situation, I felt respected but not given the means to participate as fully as those in the speaker's favor. In a democracy, representation is meant be inclusive and fair for all. More recently, female reps who didn't go along with leadership felt like teenagers left out of popularity cliques.

I also supported many well-researched and popular bills to improve life for all in the Commonwealth, but legislators never debated or voted on them because of leadership's tight control. These were issues involving small class sizes, K-grade three, to identify and do early remediation for learning challenges; ever-increasing cases of asthma in children resulting from air pollution, rodent and cockroach infestations, and chemicals used in household furnishings and products; and the need for more required palliative care training for physicians.

I enjoyed every day, serving full-time to represent my district. Because I was actively involved in legislative work and had a reputation for responding to constituent requests, my work-load increased yearly. When the unanswered emails and letters began to pile-up because I couldn't get to them with only one aide, I left the legislature.

So what can we do to bring power back to the individuals who represent us in our government, and, more importantly, back to the people of Massachusetts and to all Americans?
We can get to know political candidates by volunteering in campaigns. This way we see and experience first-hand what a candidate is all about. We can contact candidates with questions about issues important to us and expect answers to our phone calls, emails, and letters. We can also learn how responsive elected officials are by contacting their offices. They often have the ability to help constituents

cut through regulatory red-tape and can guide or connect constituents to helpful government offices. We can ask to see official votes on legislation for which we requested support. We can support and elect candidates who will work to bring the power back to the people by supporting term limits for state and federal leadership. We can support candidates who will vote for more transparency in government at all levels. This will limit the power individual leaders wield. It will also limit the influence of money in government. We can expect our elected officials to write laws that they will not be exempt from following. In the same way towns and cities are mandated to follow the Open Meeting Law, state and federal deliberations and votes should be easily accessible.

We can hold government officials to a high standard. Being in the "public eye," they have opportunities to communicate their views and actions to millions of people, young and old, through television, radio, and newspapers. Their words and actions influence the words and actions of others because of the prestige associated with their positions. We should require honesty and respect for all people from our elected officials. Our democracy depends on ensuring that our leaders live by the words in our Declaration of Independence, "We hold these truths to be self-evident, that all are created equal and endowed by their Creator with certain inalienable Rights, that among these are Life, Liberty, and the pursuit of Happiness." We can use our power of the vote to fill government with people who live up to the honor and the responsibility they receive as our representatives.

We each can and must take responsibility for doing our part in maintaining and improving our democracy. We must be willing to learn how our government is operating. Do we want government to allow giant monopolies to intimidate workers who want to unionize? Do we want our taxes paying for multinational corporate interests?

We can all do something. We can start the process with a phone call or an email that has the potential to grow into a tsunami of ordinary people working together to revive the ideals of democracy.

The power of "We the People" is strong, and we have the means to harness it for a better future for us and all who come after us!

III. Today in America, I see a lack of consensus on where to find factual news and a general distrust of media.

Back in the '50s, when I was in elementary school, we had three major television networks, and they, along with newspapers, provided voters with political information. In the '60s, the head of the Federal Communications Commission, Newt Minnow, envisioned television as a way to enhance lives through excellent educational, cultural, and media programs that enrich lives and inspire dreams. In 1967, Congress created the Corporation for Public Broadcasting (CPB) as an avenue for the continuation of non-partisan reporting of factual news. Congress funded the CPB for $445 million in 2020 which is one one-hundredth of one percent of the budget. (This amounts to a dollar and thirty-five cents per every American.) Besides this funding, these non-commercial Public Broadcasting Services (meant to educate, inform, enlighten, and enrich the public) receive donations from viewer pledges, foundations, corporate underwriting, local governments, and educational institutions. According to a nation-wide study, PBS and its member stations are the most trusted national media outlets. (Knightfoundation.org and Gallup)

With the development of Cable TV and our advanced technology has come increased access to information, most of which is created by for-profit media corporations. Biased reporting of political events, people, and issues, makes voter decision-making difficult. What we need to know to protect our Democracy is which policies benefit and which disadvantage people and who is making those policies. As we move into the future, we must identify verifiable sources for information to help us make our decisions. We also need more live media coverage of state and federal government deliberations during hearings, meetings, and formal as well as informal sessions (more C-SPAN). We need reliable internet infrastructure for consistent access to committee meetings and both formal and informal hearings that we can see on webcasts once we figure out where to find them on www.malegislature.gov/events/sessions. We need honest, factual information in order to solve our problems.

So what can we do to find agreement on factual news?

As we move into the future, we must increase funding for unbiased sources of information for making our decisions. We need access to verified public information so citizens know what is happening and can make good choices to support our Democracy.

We can demand that Congress or the Federal Communications Commission create "a set of public interest principles that will apply to broadcasting with greater transparency and consistency," (quoted from, "Revisiting the broadcast public interest standard in communications law and regulation," by Stuart Brotman, March 23, 2017, at www.brookings.edu). This will bring government actions into the open so we will know the effects of changes being made to our laws and regulations and how our tax dollars are spent.

We can again make Civics a required class for all high school graduation. Part of this curriculum should include teaching the skills for deciphering verifiable information. We can create a bi-partisan commission to develop the curriculum that will benefit future generations and us.

IV. Today in Massachusetts and throughout America, I see that we need the political will to make changes that will make life better for all. We can make politicians accountable.

Since Ronald Reagan's death in 1985, most Republican candidates have taken "No-Tax Pledges" (Grover Norquist style), and Democrats, fearing increased taxes will hurt their re-elections, have hesitated to increase taxes in this environment. Continuous reductions in state and federal revenue result in seriously neglected public infrastructure; lack of emergency preparedness for natural disasters, public health needs, and security; and inferior public service in other areas. Congressional and state legislators often give tax breaks and other benefits to take care of the rich and powerful in order to get and keep their support during elections. Large amounts of special interest money and leadership with unprecedented power will continue to operate to the detriment of our children's and grandchildren's quality of life unless we *vote* and *act* to change the status quo of how our government is run.

So what can we do to create the political will to make changes to policies that will make life better for all?
We can expect full-time representation from elected officials. Massachusetts State Representatives make a base salary of $62,500, with additional pay for leadership positions, and stipends for office needs and mileage. Their time and energy should focus on improving life for people throughout the Commonwealth.

We can let politicians know what policies we want. We can contact legislators and members of Congress by email, letter, phone call, or a visit. We can volunteer during campaigns and elections. We can check voting records. We can make politicians accountable by being active citizens. As I have heard others say, "Democracy is not a noun!" (Democracy is a government that depends on the active involvement by the whole population.)

We can communicate with public officials individually or as members of advocacy groups that share our opinions and have our best interests in mind. As I stated earlier, politicians pay attention when they hear the voices of their voters. We can vote and work for candidates we learn to respect and trust. Most politicians I encountered were good people. It's the system in which they operate that is badly broken. And we can run for public office or volunteer to help our communities in various ways. One person cannot do it all, but each of us can do something. I hope you will begin to do your part today.

Afterword: Looking to the Future

For ten years, I had the honor and privilege of driving to Beacon Hill, parking in a reserved space beneath the State House, and serving the people of Massachusetts as the State Representative from the Seventh Plymouth District.

It was exciting to work in this "City on a Hill, a place where all eyes are upon us," as Governor John Winthrop so aptly called Boston when he became the first governor of the Massachusetts Bay Colony in 1630. Like a lighthouse beacon that sits upon a hill to guide sailors safely to shore, our government leaders "are meant to be" the catalyst for guiding all people of Massachusetts to a happy, fulfilled life. In the United States, one of the richest, most powerful countries in the world, we have the expertise, the resources, and the opportunities to provide all people with a decent life, the liberty to voice different opinions, and the happiness of enjoying a long life with our loved ones. But we need the political will that will create just policies and ensure level playing fields for all of us.

During the months of the COVID-19 pandemic, we have seen, and many have experienced just how precious and fragile life is! Millions of us lost jobs and businesses, and many families continue to struggle to survive. In May 2020, we saw the eight-minute video on TV of George Floyd's murder and were reminded of the systemic racism our country has harbored for over 500 years. We have a lot to do to bring our country closer to the ideal upon which it was founded. My generation will continue to do its part to make the world more just for all, and I have great confidence that those who follow us will make it even better. Disappointed by the reality that I have become aware of, yet still optimistic, I am encouraged by the idealism and goodness of so many of my legislative colleagues, our dedicated staffs, government workers, and extremely capable, caring, and hard-working interns I had the good fortune to have in my office.

Interns fulfill the dream

My bright-eyed legislative interns, now probably close in age to mid-life, saw life the way I did when, in 1969, I graduated Bridgewater State University—whose motto is "Not to be Ministered unto, but to Minister." They were born into families of ordinary means, families with hardships and challenges, yet full of love and dreams.

During my first term, my intern from Boston College worked in a five-square-foot corner of my small office (Room 540) on the top floor of the State House. During her college summers, she mentored kids in a camp program. She went on to graduate from George Mason University Law School, earning a J.D., Magna Cum Laude. She had worked in D.C. for the U.S. Department of State, Office of International Claims and Investment Disputes, and the Department of Justice. At DOJ, she participated in pro bono and volunteer opportunities.

Another legislative intern earned a doctorate in political science and international relations and is today an assistant college professor. She co-authored a book on current issues that shape American politics and is affiliated with the Democracy in Africa Research Unit of the Center for Social Science Research at the University of Cape Town, South Africa, in conjunction with Harvard Law School. A lot of her studies focus on political behavior in new democracies. For many years she volunteered at the Pine Street Inn and at local food pantries.

A third intern volunteered with the poor in Mexico and Haiti. For her dedication to Barack Obama's presidential campaign, she had the honor of attending his inaugural activities including the inaugural ball. In 2020, this former intern participated in a worldwide bake sale to raise attention and support activism against racism.

Another of my many interns earned her Doctor of Education Leadership at Harvard and worked as a senior policy adviser for the U.S. Secretary of Education. Later, she took a position as chief of staff for the chancellor of the New York City Department of Education. (Throughout her career, she still found time to volunteer on presidential and other political campaigns.)

As you can see, these former interns, and so many others in our next generation, have the passion and dedication that it takes to bring democracy closer to the ideal of a government "of the people, by the people, and for the people." I believe the next generation will work even harder to bring government activities into the sunlight, remove special-interest money from political campaigns, support more prevention and preparedness, and create policies that will address the needs of the people of Massachusetts and throughout the country.

Every one of us has a responsibility to act in her/his individual capacity to help keep our Democracy alive and improving. Here's my take on how to do this.

Believe in yourself and get involved. As Margaret Mead said, "Never doubt that a small group of thoughtful, committed citizens can change the world. Indeed, it is the only thing that ever did." If a quiet and shy woman from a small town can stand up for the people against the tide, then anything is possible. When I was first elected, I felt insecure and inferior to some of my colleagues because I was not as educated or as proficient in public speaking as they were. However, I came to realize I had an extremely important skill for a representative: I was a listener. I believe that listening to neighbors, constituents, to the testimony of citizens and experts, to colleagues and to the information provided by advocates and lobbyists all help representatives to make better votes. Listening to one another also helps us understand each other; listening is what we all need to do to heal the division that is damaging our country. I also realized I was a very competent leader who cared about her constituents, "got into the trenches" with my staff, rolled up my sleeves, and did what was in the best interests of those I was elected to represent.

The pages of this book are not going to change our broken government system. However, I hope that in sharing my own experiences, I have helped others see how important it is for each person to do his/her part to improve the way our government works.

The first step is to register and vote. Your vote is important. A 2021 school committee and select board race in Whitman were each determined by six votes! Next, learn more about government on any level. Each town and county has a website that streams meetings on local cable TV or provides printed minutes of meetings. Volunteering for a local committee or a political campaign is a great way to learn how government works. Today, decide what you will do to change our current situation that allows power to remain in the hands of a few.

This book only skims the surface of my experiences in the Massachusetts Legislature. I treasure the hundreds more stories and the thousands more people I was proud and happy to represent. As I campaigned on every street of my three towns, Abington, East Bridgewater, and Whitman, I met wonderful people like the ones in my Harvard Street neighborhood. Probably ninety-five percent of people throughout Massachusetts, the United States, and throughout the world are good, hard-working, and honest. They want a chance to give their children a decent life.

Every day of my ten years in the legislature, I learned about life from the people I met. Even four-year-old Ava, whose artwork I received during a 2005 Head Start lobbying day at the State House, taught me something. After listening to the poem, "If I Were in Charge of the World," by Judith Viorst, Ava and her classmates drew pictures and shared a message about their world. On pink construction paper, Ava had drawn trees, flowers, and birds, and words that said: "In my world it would always be spring and things would always be growing like me. And everyone would be nice to each other—friends and help each other. And there would be no fighting." Like Ava, if I were in charge of our state, our county, and the world, everyone would be nice to each other because everyone would have equal opportunities for happiness. I would make the purpose of government be that of Hawaiian high chiefs: to have everyone succeed in living and celebrating life to the fullest. (From my readings of Richard Rohr's Daily Meditations at www.cac.org)

Appendices

1. My Democratic Opposition—Matthew Albanese was a recent Providence College graduate whose father was active in the building trade unions. Dennis Gallagher was an accounts manager who was in his late twenties, a native of East Bridgewater, and a member of the East Bridgewater Finance Committee. Dan Kelly was an active union member who worked for Bay State Gas Company. Dan's father-in-law was very involved in the popular Commercial Club of East Bridgewater.

2. My Republican Opposition—Robert Stone was a Plymouth County Commissioner and a prominent Republican who volunteered as a CCD teacher in the program I coordinated at Holy Ghost Parish. Bruce Deneen was a twenty-nine-year-old lawyer being helped by two popular former Democrats from East Bridgewater. The third Republican was Ronald Whitney, an Abington Selectman and attorney with an office in Whitman located beside his parents' business, King's Castle Land, a small amusement park and toy store. Ron was married to Caroline Regan, who had lived four houses down from where I grew up on Brigham Street in Whitman; I babysat for Caroline and her brother David when they were small. Caroline's father Denis was a former Democratic candidate for state rep whom my family had supported in the 1960s. Ron had been in my English class at Whitman-Hanson Regional High School. He was a good kid and a good student.

3. Cost of Financing a Campaign—Chris Gabrielli and Mitt Romney, two strong gubernatorial candidates in Massachusetts, were wealthy enough to contribute millions of their own money toward their campaigns. Gabrielli spent $5 million of his own money in 1998 to run for Congress, $7 million in 2002 to run for lieutenant governor, and almost $10 million in 2006 to run for governor. Mitt Romney self-funded $6 million in 2002 to run for governor and $45 million in 2008 to run for president. However, in the 2012 presidential campaign, he only donated $150,000 of his personal wealth. Kerry Healy, another wealthy Massachusetts candidate, used $9.4 million of her own money to run for governor in 2006. In the running for the December 2009 Democratic senatorial primary was Michael Pagliuca, former Baine Capital employee and owner of the Boston Celtics. Pagliuca's personal wealth amounted to over $400 million. These examples are just the tip of the iceberg of how money influences our political campaigns.

Politicians who amass millions of dollars in their campaign war chests have a great advantage over a newcomer who must expend precious campaign time each day raising the necessary funds for a campaign. Amounts grow in these war chests from year-round donations from special interest groups that want easy access to politicians who can determine the direction of our policies and where our billions of tax dollars go.

4. Gathering Signatures on Nomination Papers—I collected signatures in various places in my three towns: weekday mornings in front of the post offices, where I'd meet small business owners, retirees, and young mothers; Saturday mornings at the East Bridgewater Recycling Center (formerly, the town dump), where I met environmentally conscious families; early mornings at the Abington and Whitman train stations, to greet white-collar commuters on their way to Boston; Friday evenings in front of Hollywood Video (for VCR movie rentals); Curtis Liquors in Whitman, to meet workers happy to begin their weekend with a little relaxation; and on weekends, I asked for signatures when door-knocking in all three towns. It wasn't always easy. Some people saw my clipboard and avoided me like the plague—hurrying into the post office without making eye contact or pretending they didn't hear my request. Some said I shouldn't be on government property and complained to the postmaster. Collecting nomination signatures at the post office was permitted as long as I didn't bother people or stand too close to the entrance. Some days were cloudy and cold; others were warm and humid. The majority of people were friendly and respectful whether they signed my papers or not. Candidates for office should not be discouraged by cold-shoulder reactions they encounter. And before starting to collect signatures on nomination papers, I advise reading the following information that I learned from personal experience and the experiences of colleagues.

To run for a seat in the Massachusetts House of Representatives, a person must be eighteen years of age or older, a registered voter, and have lived in the district he/she wants to represent for a full year prior to the election. No education requirement bars participation, no previous experience requirement, no mandatory background check, and no exam to pass. Of course, however, all candidates' personal information and more becomes public information during a campaign. It was important for me to collect more than150 signatures from people who lived in my district and get them to the Town Clerk's Office ahead of the deadline. It's important to follow all the rules for collecting nomination signatures: A signer must be a voter, registered as a member of the candidate's party or as an unenrolled voter. The signature must be in either black or blue ink and consist of the person's full name as recorded when he/she registered to vote. The voter's correct street address is also needed. Extraneous marks on the paper and incomplete or incorrect information in the shaded area at the top of the paper can nullify a whole sheet of signatures. Election Registrars in a candidate's district must certify signatures before nomination papers go to the Secretary of State. In Massachusetts, a potential candidate's 150 signatures must be in the Secretary of State's Election Division in the McCormick Building by 5 p.m. on the designated date in April or the date designated before a Special

Election. Some incumbents have missed the deadline, and as a result, had to run as a write-in.

It's important to collect many more than the 150 signatures and have them submitted to the town clerk's office early for several reasons. Some signatures may not be valid because people may forget to re-register when they move, or they may be too embarrassed to say they aren't registered. Others may be registered in another political party.

5. Pharmacy Assessment in Outside Section of Annual Budget—Below I have copied a section from our budget verbatim so you can get an idea of the complicated legalese with which proposed budgets and legislation are written.

Chapter 184 of the Acts of 2002, House Budget, Outside Section 101 -Section 26. (a) For the purposes of this section, the following terms shall have the following meanings:
"Assessment," for all pharmacies, an amount assessed upon each non-Medicare and non-Medicaid prescription dispensed by the pharmacies.
"Pharmacy," any retail drug business registered by the board of registration in pharmacy in accordance with chapter 112 that is authorized to dispense controlled substances, including, retail drug businesses as defined in section 1 of chapter 94C.
(b) Each pharmacy shall pay an assessment upon each non-Medicare and non-Medicaid prescription dispensed to the division quarterly. The assessment shall be sufficient in the aggregate to generate $36 million in each fiscal year. The assessment shall be implemented as a broad-based health care-related fee as defined in 42 U.S.C. {1396b (w)(3)(B). The division may promulgate regulations that authorize the assessment of interest on any unpaid liability at a rate not to exceed an annual percentage rate of 18 per month. The receipts from the assessment, any federal financial participation received by the

commonwealth as a result of expenditures funded by these assessments and late fees at a rate not to exceed 5 per cent per assessment and interest thereon shall be credited to the Health Care Security Trust Fund established by chapter 29D.

(c) The commissioner shall prepare a form on which each pharmacy shall report quarterly its total prescriptions dispensed and shall calculate the assessment due. The commissioner shall distribute the forms to each pharmacy at least annually. The failure to distribute the form or the failure to receive a copy of the form shall not stay the obligation to pay the assessment by the date specified herein.

(d) The division shall have the authority to inspect and copy the records of a pharmacy for purposes of auditing its calculation of the assessment. In the event that the division determines that a pharmacy has either overpaid or underpaid the assessment, the division shall notify the pharmacy of the amount due or refund the overpayment. The division may impose per diem penalties if a nursing home fails to produce documentation as requested by the division.

(e) In the event that a pharmacy is aggrieved by a decision of the division that an assessment was underpaid by such pharmacy, the pharmacy may file an appeal to the division of administrative law appeals within 60 days of the date of the notice of underpayment or the date the notice was received, whichever is later. The division of administrative law appeals shall conduct each appeal as an adjudicatory proceeding pursuant to chapter 30A and a pharmacy aggrieved by a decision of the division of administrative law appeals shall be entitled to judicial review pursuant to section 14 of chapter 30A.

(f) The commissioner may enforce the provisions of this section by notifying the department of public health of unpaid assessments. Within 45 days after notice to a pharmacy of amounts due, the department may revoke licensure of a pharmacy that fails to remit delinquent fees.

(g) The division shall quarterly determine the amount of MassHealth services to be funded by the assessment and shall provide written notice of such amount to the comptroller before the first business day of each quarter. The comptroller shall transfer from the Health Care Security Trust Fund, established pursuant to section 1 of chapter 29D, to the Health Care Quality Improvement Trust Fund, on the first business day of each quarter the amount indicated by the division, but in no event shall such transfer exceed $72,000,000 in fiscal year 2003.

(h) The division, in consultation with the division of medical assistance, shall promulgate regulations necessary to implement this section.

6. Informal Sessions and Suspending the Rules—The main purpose of informal sessions is to move things along in the legislative process. They allow bills to move to various committees, and sometimes a bill, with or without amendments, is passed or defeated unanimously with a voice vote when only a handful of members are present in the House or Senate Chamber. These rules, as mentioned earlier, are voted on by members of each legislative body at the beginning of each two-year session for organizing itself and carrying out business.

The following language is the rule allowing informal sessions, and is quoted from the Manual for the General Court, the book of rules with which the Massachusetts Legislature functions: House Rule 44 The Speaker may designate when an informal session of the House shall be held, provided said Speaker gives notice of such informal session at a prior session of the House. The Speaker may, in cases of emergency, cancel a session or declare any session of the House to be an informal session. At an informal session the House shall only consider reports of committees, papers from the Senate, bills for enactment or resolves for final passage, bills containing emergency preambles and the matters in the Orders of the Day. Motions to reconsider moved at such informal session shall be placed in the Orders of the Day for the succeeding day, and no new business shall be entertained, except by unanimous consent. Formal debate,

or the taking of the sense of the House by yeas and nays, shall not
be conducted during such informal session. Upon the receipt of a
petition signed by at least a majority of the members elected to the
House, so requesting, the Speaker shall, when the House is meeting
in informal session under the provisions of Joint Rule 12A, designate
a formal session, to be held within seven days of said receipt, for the
purpose of considering the question of passage of a bill, notwith-
standing the objections of the Governor, returned pursuant to Article
2, Section 1, Clause 1, Part 2 of the Massachusetts Constitution. This
rule shall not be suspended unless by unanimous consent of the members present.

The key words there are "unanimous consent of the members
present." Typically, there aren't many members present at informal
sessions (sometimes just a handful) so it's easy to have unanimous
consent. The result is that a few people can wield enormous power.
An informal vote is taken when only leadership (the Speaker or
his designee) and other representatives who "happen" to attend the
session are present. It only takes one person to object and keep a bill
from going forward. On the other hand, a bill can be graveled through
without debate unless someone objects. Unfortunately, some questionable legislation can be decided in these informal sessions.

7. The Oral Health Issue Brief of the Massachusetts Health Policy
Forum, June 16, 2009 (https://heller.brandeis.edu/mass-health-policy-
forum/categories/oral-health/pdfs/improving-oral-health-across-the-
commonwealth/putting-mouth-back-body-issue-brief.pdf) — This
report, "Putting the Mouth Back in the Body," details how oral health
is critical to overall health, the progress Massachusetts has made in
providing care, and what challenges lie ahead. As a result of poor
dental health, people suffer with pain, low self-esteem, poor nutrition, loss of work and school days, and reduced social engagement.
While we made progress in access to dental care, there were gaps in
those receiving the care, including the elderly and people in nursing

homes. As dentists in the "baby boomer" generation retire, we may face a future shortage of dentists.

8. NPR 2017 Book of the Year: *Teeth: The Story of Beauty, Inequality, and the Struggle for Oral Health in America*, written by Mary Otto, an American medical journalist. (The New Press, 2017)

9. It took a few years and the foresight and dedication of East Bridgewater residents to determine the specific use of this land as a public benefit. The results today are: The Center at Sachem Rock, a senior and community center (355 Plymouth Street) available for public rentals. Surrounding the Center are thirty-two acres of Sachem Farm land, which are now part of the Nunckatesset Greenway Project, a 21st century greenway project linking major parks and open spaces throughout New England and the United States. See www.umass.edu for details about the New England Greenway. Howard Wilbur, my constituent who first introduced me to the Bay Circuit project in 1999, now in his eighties, is involved in this Greenway Project!

10. The ballot initiative or ballot question is a tool Massachusetts citizens can use to express their opinions to the legislature, seek to amend the state constitution, or propose a new state law. (The ballot initiative was first used in Massachusetts in 1920 to exclude beer and cider from the liquor prohibition law.) A ballot initiative begins with ten voters signing an initiative petition and then submitting it to the Commonwealth's attorney general and the secretary of state for review and conversion into the proper ballot question format. Then proponents must collect certified voter signatures that equal at least three percent of the total number of people voting in the previous gubernatorial election. (That meant over 50,000 signatures were collected for the 1998 Clean Elections Ballot Initiative.) These signatures must be filed with the secretary of state by a certain deadline in order for the question to be printed on the ballot. If an initiative for a new law or an advisory is voted in the affirmative, the state legislature will then consider possible amendments to the initiative and budgeting of funds necessary for its enforcement.

About the Author

Kathleen (Kathy) Teahan was born in 1947 and lived most of her life in Whitman, Massachusetts. She is a Baby Boomer and a child of the "Greatest Generation," the generation that sacrificed so much for America and the world. Inspired by her late husband Bob Teahan, Kathy entered politics in 1995. She had no personal ambitions and no axe to grind. Her memoir is a story from the heart of a woman whose purpose throughout her ten years in the Massachusetts Legislature was and is to help people. Her memoir is a yearning for courageous leadership necessary to protect and improve our Democracy.

Kathy previously published a children's book (2017), *The Cookie Loved 'Round the World*, that tells the story of the famous Toll House chocolate chip cookie invented in Whitman by Ruth Wakefield.

Teahan currently lives in Harwich Port, Massachusetts.

Look for Kathy's website: www.KathleenTeahan.com.

Acknowledgments

Although I began this memoir in 2008, it came to fruition thanks to the encouragement and assistance of many people. Thank you to the people of Abington, East Bridgewater, and Whitman who gave their time, energy, and votes to provide me with the experiences I recall in this memoir.

Thank you to my friend John C. Edwards (no relation to the 2008 presidential candidate) for his kind encouragement and support for this memoir. Thank you to my high school classmate Joe Kuzborski and his wife Joanne for their beta reading and Joanne's generosity in typing and formatting earlier drafts as well as her many inspirations throughout the process.

I owe a debt of gratitude to Marjorie Turner Holman (www.marjorieturner.com), my developmental editor, coach and publishing advisor, who greatly improved my manuscript's clarity and patiently supported me in the completion of this book. I am truly grateful to the writers I met in the Cape Cod Community College Academy for Lifelong Learning's memoir class, who inspired me to publish my memories. My sincere thanks to Francie King (www.historykeep.com), for identifying where to provide more details or explanations and for her meticulous editing. Many thanks to Christy Bailey, who graciously volunteered her editing skills and did a final read before publication. Thank you to Pamela Johnson (TechproPublications.com) who brought my book to completion with her outstanding book and cover design.

Thank you to Patrick Derosier (CPU Guys, Inc., Hanson), computer technologist and grandson of Ellen Callanan, for rescuing me during computer disasters. Thank you to John Campbell (Harding Print, Whitman) for print and format consultations during my legislative and my writing careers. Thank you to Thomas O'Brien, Plymouth County Treasurer and my legislative colleague, for studying and saving all copies of our Manual for the General Court. Thank you to my friend Michelle Caywood for the "About the Author" photo. Thank you to Health Care for All, for my 2003 award, "For the People, Against the Tide," the only award displayed in my home, and the inspiration for my book's title. Thank you to Alan White for his humor that inspired the "lapping tide."

Thank you to Allison Staton and all advocates who worked tirelessly for at-risk children, elders, and families. My sincere gratitude to Myron Allukian, DDS, Carol Donavan, Michael Dukakis, Alan French, Jay Kaufman, Howard Koh, MD, Professor Michael Kryzanek, Christine Maiorano, David Mulligan, Deval Patrick, and Denise Provost, all of whom wrote kind words about me and my book. Each of them has been a leader who did much to improve our world, and each one helped me contribute my small piece to a brighter future.

Lastly, big thank you to my seven siblings, my four children and their spouses for all they gave to my campaigns in so many ways, and for all their love. Most importantly, thank you to all who read *For the People, Against the Tide* and then do their part to move us closer to a more just and peaceful world.

www.ingramcontent.com/pod-product-compliance
Lightning Source LLC
Chambersburg PA
CBHW050727030426
42336CB00012B/1447